Closing the Round-the-World Circle

Anne E. Brevig

Published in cooperation with Halvor Nome, Nome Design & Publishing,
Halden, Norway

ISBN: 1494313693
ISBN-13: 978-1494313692

DEDICATION

To Martin

and the

People we met on the Way.

Dare to take the leap –
Dolphins will carry you

Honorine Hermelin

CONTENTS

PREFACE

At the peak of their careers, Anne Brevig and Martin Vennesland made the decision of their lives: they chose freedom and a highly uncertain future on the high seas instead of secure jobs and the safety and comfort of life ashore.

In order to finance their dream, they sold their house and most of their belongings and moved onboard their 40-foot sailboat. It became their one and only home for 15 years. Neither imagined that they were going to spend 9 years on the 7 seas and journey more than 56,000 nautical miles. Back on terra firma, their once-in-a-lifetime adventure, which was packed with drama and excitement, was immortalized in a beautiful coffee table book, "9 Years on the 7 Seas". It quickly became a bestseller, and when it sold out in paper format, the adventurous couple decided to share their experiences with the world in the equally exciting "Seven Seas Adventures" Series, which is now available both in print and several eBook formats.

Anne and Martin's blue water adventure is not about breaking any records. Its main focus is meeting people from different backgrounds and cultures - encounters that take on entirely different dimensions when sailing off the beaten track far away from the traditional tourist routes.

Anne and Martin crossed the big oceans and visited 76 countries and island nations. They realized their dreams. Now, they hope that their books in the "Seven Seas Adventures" Series, which are saturated with enchanting encounters, danger and unique experiences, will inspire others to pursue their own dreams – whatever they may be. At least, to "dare to take the leap". The Series certainly gives a rare opportunity to live vicariously in theirs, and their beloved sailboat, "NOR SIGLAR'S" wake.

ABOUT THIS BOOK

In the last book in Seven Seas Adventure Series, we encounter some of the toughest and most dangerous challenges of our entire voyage, testing our endurance to its absolute limit, while at the same time experiencing exhilarating highs.

We are guided by the stars across the normally benign Indian Ocean. We get caught in a gigantic commercial fish net in the pitch black of a stormy night, the most dangerous and life-threatening episode of our entire voyage.

We sail through the pirate infested waters of the Gulf of Aden, where, a catamaran sailing alone ahead of us is attacked and boarded, the wife shot in the leg, and just about everything they own, except the boat, is stolen.

We join a flotilla and sail non-stop through the Strait of Bab el Mandeb, the "Gate of Tears" on the Horn of Africa, into the dreaded Red Sea to the poor and destitute countries of Eritrea and Sudan. We explore the mysteries of the Arab world with its golden mosques and pencil thin minarets, muezzins calling to prayer, veiled women in flowing, black abayas huddled in groups, souks overflowing with exotic dates, herbs and spices, fragrant perfumes and gold, frankincense and myrrh of Biblical times.

We dress as the locals, tour the desert with armed guards, visit girl's schools and drink sweet tea with qat-chewing locals. In Eritrea, we meet the descendents of King Solomon and the Queen of Sheba. We sample local specialties in humble one-room homes.

In Sudan, we explore the many beautiful desert anchorages, witness poverty beyond belief, and visit the last slave trading post in the world.

Then, it's off to Egypt with its impressive pharaohs and pyramids, ancient sites of Valley of the Kings and Luxor. We battle our way to the safety of the Suez Canal where infamous pilots nag us for baksheesh, bribes and such.

In Israel, where we cross our course from four years prior and can call ourselves Circumnavigators. We receive a hero's welcome and even meet Shimon Peres! We take the fast track through the Mediterranean where we have been twice before. At the Strait of Gibraltar, we point our bow north to finish in Norway.

THE INDIAN OCEAN - RED SEA
AND THE MEDITERRANEAN

THE MALDIVES – THE ARABIAN PENINSULA

Headwinds on the Indian Ocean? At this time of year? Impossible! But that's exactly what we got the first three nights out: wind from the northnorthwest. Gale force, no less. And a current that pushed us west. We had to sail hard on the wind. Even so, it didn't take long before we were way off course. We had to tack. Back and forth. Disappointing when you expect a pleasant passage with the wind on the beam. Between January and March, the northeast monsoon blows steadily on the Indian Ocean. It is the best time for the crossing to the Red Sea. The old seafarers knew to take advantage of the monsoons, which alter direction according to season. But that was not to be for us. Thankfully we have a fast boat that sails well into the wind.

Gradually, the wind veered towards the northeast and moderated enough that we could shake out the reefs and keep a reasonable course. Life became comfortable onboard. There was no shortage of diversion. In the mornings, the deck was littered with flying fish. But they were so small and smelled so foul that we were not tempted to fry them for breakfast like the "old salts" did. In the daytime, we enjoyed watching schools of dolphins frolicking around the bow and thousands of tuna performing spectacular leaps into midair. At night, we were guided by the Big Dipper in the north, the Southern Cross in the south and Orion directly above. Never before had we seen so much phosphorescence in the sea. It was chock full of plankton that sparkled, glittered and shone, turning the whole ocean into one big fireworks.

We were moving into unsafe waters: Somalia, Yemen and Oman

to the west-northwest, Iran and Pakistan to the north and India to the east. The further north we went, the more anxious we felt. And it didn't help matters when we heard that a sailboat had been attacked in the Gulf of Aden. The cruisers became jittery. We established the "Red Sea-Indian Ocean Cruisers' Net" to keep track of each other. About 30 sailboats participated in the net. It was reassuring to be close to the cruising family in such troubled waters. The net was also a good way to exchange weather information in an area where no other forecasting service was available.

Indian Ocean sunset.

One morning, an Englishman reported that he had been followed during the night. Half a dozen 20-25 metre long wooden dhows had come after him from different directions. Kotic changed course and increased his speed to 8.5 knots. The powered dhows chased him for a couple of miles before giving up. They had been close enough that he could see some men on the bow. It looked like they were planning to board him. But he did not think they were armed. So it was impossible to know what their intentions were. The episode frightened everyone in the sailing community. Few could motor as fast as Kotic and have the ability to outrun a large powered vessel.

After this incident, similar reports kept coming in from the same waters. But nobody was attacked. It would appear that there was a fishing fleet in a 10-12 mile radius around 13° N and 60° E. Most likely, they were only fishermen who wanted to see if they could scare or get something from the "rich yachties". But you never know. Besides, we were getting closer to Socotra, an island off the coast of Somalia notorious for piracy attacks on boats that came too near. So we were startled by a call on the emergency channel: "Tourist boat! Tourist Boat!" Was someone calling us? We didn't see anybody around. Should we answer? I didn't think so. "Why not?" Martin asked. I was afraid it could be a trap. Better to avoid questions that could lead to a possible confrontation. If we were asked for help, we were, according to maritime law, obliged to comply. But why in the world were they calling a "tourist boat"? Martin felt they might have a warning of some sort. In that case, wouldn't a professional mariner make a standard "securité" call?

Before we could reach a conclusion, Cormoran, a British ketch about 20 nautical miles behind us answered. That triggered a well of questions: "Where you from?" Cormoran: "Ireland." Caller: "England?" Cormoran: "No. Ireland. Where are you from?" Caller: "Iran. How many people on your boat?" Cormoran did not reply. After some unintelligible chatter in the background, the Iranian returned: "You speak Arabic?" Cormoran: "No. Never been to an Arabic country. What language do you speak?" "Arabic, Iranian and Somali. Me English no good." Cormoran: "Better than my Arabic. Are you a fishing boat?" More mumbling. "What your position?" Cormoran declined to answer. Long pause. Then the Iranian announced: "Me position: 13°46′ N, 60°10′ E." End of conversation.

His position was in the exact same area where Kotic and several other sailboats had been chased. It was only 12 nautical miles ahead. We did not like that the Iranian wanted to know how many people Cormoran had onboard. So we dropped the cruising spinnaker and rolled out the genoa to sail harder on the wind in order to get by the troubled waters as quickly as possible. As darkness fell, we refrained from using our navigation lights to avoid being seen. But we neither heard, nor saw anybody. So that was the end of the intermezzo. Again, they were probably only curious fishermen. Maybe they just wanted to practice their English? Were all the rumours making us so nervous that we made a big number of nothing?

Five days out of Uligamu, we reached the halfway point. That night, it blew up from the northwest again. We put two reefs in the mainsail and furled in half the genoa. At midnight, just before change of watch, I noticed a strange vibration in the boat. Suddenly, the sails started fluttering and slamming like mad and the speed dropped from 6 to 1.5 knots. I didn't understand a thing. The compass turned 180 degrees and the waves came crashing across the transom. Martin was up in a flash. "What's going on?" he cried confused, rubbing the sleep from his eyes. Then we both saw it at the same time: a gigantic "V" sparkling in the phosphorescence behind us. We were caught in an enormous fishnet!

Automatically, Martin grabbed the paddle of the wind vane to save it from getting torn off by the net. Hitting his head, he just about lost his glasses in the process. Blood was streaming down his face. Nor Siglar was bucking and heaving like mad. She was virtually at a standstill in the steep seas, waves washing into the cockpit soaking us to the bones. The strong commercial fishnet must have been several kilometres long. It was pulling and tugging so hard at the boat that we thought it was going to tear both rudder and propeller right off. And the enormous stress on the rudderpost could easily break the hull open. It was not hard to imagine what would happen to us then in the middle of the Indian Ocean.

We were in serious trouble. It was decidedly the most dangerous situation we had experienced. For the first time ever, we were truly scared. We needed help. At any cost. Ignoring the piracy danger, we sent out an emergency call. But there was no reply. We had to manage on our own. First, we had to get the sails down. And that was not an easy matter in 30-knot following winds on a surface that was in constant motion. But miracles happen. We made it. The next step was to get untangled from the fishnet. It was impossible to reach it from the deck. And there was no way Martin could dive into the pitch-black turbulent waters to cut us loose under those circumstances. We had to do it from the deck. "I can't hold it with the boat hook," Martin called in despair. "It's too heavy. We've got to get it closer to the hull somehow."

We attached some big fishhooks to a rope, caught the net and tried to winch it closer that way. But the hooks were not strong enough. They ripped right out. We never thought of using the little dinghy anchor. That would have worked. But we didn't think clearly in the panic. Finally, we spliced two broom handles together and lashed a long sharp knife to the end. With a superhuman effort, Martin managed to hold the net long enough with the boat hook for me to reach it with the knife by lying flat on my stomach and leaning out over the gunwales and the roaring sea. The edge of the fishnet was tight as a violin string and snapped the minute the knife touched it. What a relief! As the net gave way, it felt as though all of Nor Siglar relaxed. Our first crisis was almost resolved. But what now? What if the rudder and propeller were damaged?

Half the night was gone before we managed to get ourselves free. We had been totally absorbed in what we were doing and had not noticed that several fishing boats had arrived in the meantime. We were surrounded by lights! How were we going to get ourselves out of this maze unscathed? We were terrified of getting caught in another unlit fishnet. So we sailed short distances back and forth on the same course until daylight.

Once more we got caught in something but lost it again after a few 360-degree turns. Our nerves were clearly fraught and our imaginations working overtime. For when we heard a strange rattling sound, we thought the propeller was falling off. But it only turned out to be some empty bottles that had fallen over and were rolling around in the lazarette.

As dawn was breaking, we got away as quickly as we could, worried that the fishermen would discover that we had cut their net, and then, perhaps come after us. Fortunately, the wind had changed to a more easterly direction so we could hoist the cruising spinnaker again. Later that day, we discovered a tear in the mainsail. Where was this going to end? We seemed to be caught in a vicious circle. Martin, dejected and sporting a big bandage around his head, exclaimed: "There's got to be a limit to what we have to go through before this is all over! I am getting sick and tired of it!"

We knew we didn't have far to go when the offshore wind Belat blew up and filled the air with sand and dust from the Arabian Peninsula and terns and frigates settled down on the spreaders. Finally, after eleven stressful days, it was a huge relief to reach Oman and the safety of the ultra modern port of Mina Raysut just west of Salalah. The anchor was barely down before we dove in to inspect the damage. Only a few bits of fishnet remained tangled around the shaft. Apart from a small nick in the rudder, nothing was damaged.

Nor Siglar had done it again!

The Indian Ocean did not live up to our expectations. But now, that crossing was behind us as well. And it is strange how quickly one forgets. Once in calm waters, the challenges at sea are soon forgotten and you are ready to start all over again. What is really interesting is that when something so dramatic happens, you discover new qualities about yourself. Qualities you are unaware of. Being alone, far away from civilization, you only have yourself to trust. You have to be able to tackle whatever comes along. In this case, we both discovered a strength we never knew we had.

PROSPEROUS OMAN AND IMPOVERISHED YEMEN

"Allah Akbar! Allah Akbar!" Dawn was just breaking as the muezzin on the Navy ship in the harbour started summoning the faithful to prayer. The call, often dubbed the "Muslim alarm clock", woke us up setting the tone for our first day in Oman.

We received a one-week visa to explore this nouveau-riche oil country where the camel, the "Bedouin's Best Friend," still reigns supreme. Camel breeding is a lucrative business and racing extremely popular. Apparently, a first class camel can be as valuable as a Rolls Royce. Consequently, it is quite a status symbol and a popular trading item. You can even get a woman for a couple of camels in this world where you not only receive a substantial fine, but a jail term as well, if you hit a camel crossing the road. Should you happen to do the same to a woman, you would only get a small fine! Or so we were told. No wonder cars slowed down when camels were near.

Oman is truly a land of contrasts where macho men in kummar caps, muzzar turbans and bright white dishdasha robes race around in modern 4x4's on dusty roads crowded with goats, camels and "Ship of the Desert" warning signs. During the daytime, there were almost only men to be seen. Women did not appear until dark. Moving around in groups, completely covered in flowing black cloaks with only a narrow slit revealing mysterious eyes, they looked like ghosts to us. Having finished their chores of the day, they gathered in the women's souq. It was overflowing with exotic products like dates, herbs and spices, fragrant perfumes, gold, frankincense and myrrh. During Biblical times, Saudi Arabia became wealthy from the trade of the valuable frankincense - the dried sap of the endemic Boswellia tree. On our way to the local gardens, we relived a bit of history, visiting the Prophet Job's Tomb and the ruins of one of the Queen of Sheba's many palaces.

Omanis in dazzling white dishdashas. How can they stay so neat and clean in the perpetual desert dust?

Since the U.K. educated Sultan Qaboos bin Said Al Said deposed his father in 1970, Oman has gone through extensive reforms. So it is a modern country. At least by local standards. Salalah's first Internet café opened while we were there. In fact, I was the first client. I must admit that it was rather odd to be served by data specialists in Biblical attire.

We had long been fretting about the Gulf of Aden and the Strait of Bab el Mandeb on the Horn of Africa. This was where a sailboat had been attacked recently. The couple were sailing by themselves when five armed pirates from Somalia boarded and robbed their catamaran, wounding the wife with a gunshot to her leg. The year before, a Finnish couple was attacked in the same area. That time, the pirates were not satisfied with money and equipment only. They took the boat and the couple hostage as well. Several months later, after considerable suffering and despair, the Finns were released. They got their boat back in return for a large sum of money. By that time, however, their boat was in shreds.

So rumours flourished. The cruisers discussed at length how we could get by these dangerous waters safely. The conclusion was to sail in convoy, 5-6 nautical miles off the coast of Yemen. The local police were known to be involved in piracy activities, regularly scanning the radio frequencies for cruisers' locations. So we were afraid to reveal our exact latitude and longitude to each other on the net. We created waypoints with code names like "Henry Morgan" (Aden) and "Blackbird" (Bal el Mandeb). This way, we could report our position as "x" nautical miles from the coastline and "y" nautical miles from the waypoint in question. The transmissions had to be short. Women were not allowed on the air. A female voice would be a dead give-away of an offshore cruiser.

The ocean was calm as a mirror when we left Salalah. Just as well. It was easier to stay together when everyone was using the engine. A few boats approached us on the way. But no one bothered us, probably because we were part of a group. Our strategy worked. Three tense days later, we arrived safely in Al Mukalla, a few hundred miles east of Aden. The Friday prayer was in full swing with muezzins calling from half a dozen minarets, the echoes competing in the hills.

Captivated by a spectacular sunset on ochre coloured cliffs, and swinging peacefully at anchor, we were startled by a knock on the hull. It was the officials who wanted to check us in. Due to recent kidnappings of tourists, a curfew was in effect: we had to be back on the boat by 9 o'clock at night. We also had to relinquish our passports in exchange for a three-day visitor's permit; barely enough to get a taste of the realm of the legendary Queen of Sheba, who was so powerful about 3000 years ago.

A young Yemenite poses with is keffiya.

On an outing to the countryside, we were accompanied by soldiers armed with machine guns. They were protecting us from kidnappers, they said. Time and again, we were stopped at military checkpoints and interrogated. Not understanding a word, we were rather intimidated. We did not at all feel safe in this country, which had been ravaged by civil war for two decades. Although Yemen is unified now, the political situation is still unstable. Watchtowers of sun-dried clay, half finished mud and brick houses and military compounds partially camouflaged by cement walls dominate the dry and desolate landscape. Unlike Oman, there were

It feels like history is turned back 1000 years at this main road near Al ukhalla.

no camels to be seen, for Yemen is an impoverished land. Most people live from subsistence farming and fishing. And when shepherds crossed the road right in front of our car with their herds, then wandered off into the hostile desert amidst thorny shrubs, we felt as though we were a thousand years back in time.

Like their sisters in Oman, the women in Yemen were dressed in black from head to toe. However, they were out and about during daylight hours and seemed much more open and liberal.

Muslim girls in sewing class.

They certainly did not avoid us when we tried to make contact. "Our dress is not a sign of oppression like you think in the west," an animated young woman explained. She was keen to practise her English. "It is a sign of modesty. Every woman with respect for herself and Allah wears the abaya, hijab and burqa. Mine are the latest fashion from Paris!" she joked as she made a coquettish pirouette on high-heeled shoes swinging an elegant Gucci handbag on her arm.

Later, I just had to try the Islamic dress. It made me feel like I had lost my identity. I couldn't help but think that that was exactly the intention in this male-dominated society. From the anchorage, Al Mukalla looked like a scenic town with its picturesque façade of cream coloured Moorish buildings, mosques and minarets. On closer inspection, however, the "white city" was far from it. Paper, junk and plastic were scattered all over the place.

The smell of sewage penetrated the air. Sheep, goats, cats and chickens were rummaging around narrow alleys and steep lanes. But the place had an infectious atmosphere. In the evening, the men flocked to the mosques. Afterwards, they spilled out on the sidewalk where they sat till late at night, sipping piping hot sweet tea in small glasses, their cheeks bulging from chewing qat, a mildly stimulating fresh leaf, as they were playing their games of domino and cards.

Nor Siglar's crew in local garb.

The restaurants were for men only. However, an exception was made for tourists. So the last evening in Yemen, we went out to dinner. It was quite an experience. At the entrance, there was a tap of running water for rinsing hands before and after the meal. Bread was used in lieu of cutlery. We watched as flat disks of the unleavened bread were baked plastered against the side of a glowing hot clay cylinder. Copying the locals, we broke the flatbread into pieces and scooped up different kinds of dips and the fish, which was fried whole and served on a newspaper. It was delicious. In the absence of "Ladies", I had to use the "Men's". That was a mixed pleasure. The adjoining room was full of prayer mats readily available to patrons and staff.

It was nearly two months since the end of Ramadan, and Eid-al-Adha, the "Feast of Sacrifice", was near. Next to us in the anchorage, a big dhow was lying dangerously low in the water. It was full of goats! They had been shipped from Somalia to be slaughtered for the three-day celebration, which marks the end of the Muslims' annual Pilgrimage to Mecca. We could probably expect to meet many such craft on our way to the Red Sea. No doubt, we would mistake them for pirates.

THE DREADED RED SEA

It was time to tackle the infamous Red Sea, every sailor's nightmare. The long and narrow inland sea is known for its notoriously strong northerly winds. Usually blowing days on end, the persistent headwinds can make the voyage north a real test of endurance. Especially if one is in a hurry. However, if one is prepared to wait for weather windows, the Red Sea can be a great experience. The distance from Bab el Mandeb on the Horn of Africa in the south to Suez in the north is about 1,200 nautical miles. Under normal circumstances, a sailboat can cover such a stretch in a couple of weeks. But not in the Red Sea. Unless willing to face a lot of discomfort, one should allow 6-8 weeks for the transit.

The best time to sail north is from February to May, a period when the unforgiving northerlies are at their weakest. We were right on schedule. On February 29, we left Al Mukalla for the 600 nautical mile passage to Massawa halfway up the Eritrean coast. We were still in pirate-infested waters, so our little flotilla stayed together along the rugged coast. Two uneventful days later, outside the port of Aden, the other boats wanted to go in and top up their fuel and water supplies. We had plenty to reach Eritrea, so since the weather was benign, we decided to continue on our own. We stayed parallel to the shipping lane where we should be able to get help if necessary. At one point, someone started cursing, swearing and calling obscenities on the emergency channel. What kind of people would do that? Was the foul language intended for us? It was rather scary and not very pleasant to listen too. We did not see anybody to whom the profanities could be traced.

Fortunately, nothing came of the incident. A day later, we left the Gulf of Aden behind for good and sailed in through Bab el Mandeb, also called the Gate of Tears. Large military installations in both Yemen and Djibouti guard both sides of the 27 km wide strait

Sawakin mosque.

separating eastern Africa and the Arabian Peninsula. The pass, as well as the southern part of the Red Sea, is reputed for its strong southerly winds that can blow up to gale force strength without much notice and cause dangerous waves. However, our transit became a real anti climax. Not a breath of wind - and glassy calm seas!

Despite busy freighter traffic, we chose to sail up the centre of the Red Sea rather than risking unfriendly encounters with the hostile military closer to shore. In fact, we did not want to stop until we reached Massawa. The ports on the way were reputed to be unsafe due to border conflicts and local strife. We also kept a safe distance from the Hanish Islands, which were disputed by Yemen and Eritrea. Sailboats anchored in the lee of the islands had been shot at recently. The Eritrean port of Asad was also to be avoided. For here, innocent sailors accused of being spies have been taken hostage from time to time.

Before long, the Red Sea lived up to its reputation. Despite a peaceful introduction, we were soon clobbered by fierce southerly winds and the highest waves we have ever seen. After a few days of exhilarating surfing, the wind abruptly veered to the north. We put two reefs in the main - and didn't shake them out until we reached Suez two months later.

WAR-TORN ERITREA

After a stressful six-day passage from Al Mukalla, we were relieved to arrive safely in the war-torn port of Massawa where the ruins and destruction from bombing were clearly visible. Despite this the port was well-organized and the check-in formalities went surprisingly well, considering the devastated condition of the country. We even received permission to stay for a whole month. For the first time, we had to sign a document that we did not have any stowaways onboard.

As usual after a longer trip, we were exhausted and retired early. We were just about to doze off when we heard a gentle knock on the hull. "Hello! Need some help?" A kind-looking man of slight build was standing alongside in his small makeshift pram. "My name is Solomon," the soft-spoken man said, reaching his hand over the railing in greeting. "I have a donkey and a cart and can get you diesel and water." This was how a pleasant relationship started with a proud representative of Eritrea's friendly population. Solomon was not only an enterprising and hardworking man. He was knowledgeable as well, and more than willing to share his wisdom.

"I am named after our famed ancestor," he declared in reasonable English. "Eritreans are descendents from the legendary union between King Solomon and the Queen of Sheba." Giving us a short summary of the nation's history, he recalled with a sigh: "I was only 12 years old when Massawa fell to Ethiopia during a Soviet-supported air raid in 1977. My family lost everything. Then came the drought followed by poor harvests, hunger and starvation in the 80's." The mild-mannered man was very thin. "I am not used to eating very much," he said. "We are very poor. But we are not starving any more. Life has not been easy. But now we are anticipating a better future," he concluded. "By the way, we'll never give Ethiopia access to the Red Sea!" he added as an afterthought. That was a comment we heard often during our short stay.

Haile Selassie's summer palace in Massawa.

We remained at anchor for almost two weeks in the large well protected lagoon-type harbour, which commanded a dramatic view of the ruins of past Emperor Haile Selassie's bombed out summer palace. We were shocked at the terrible destruction and all the men hobbling around on crutches. Many had amputated arms and legs. So our first impression was not very uplifting. The Eritreans, however, were the nicest, most positive people imaginable. It was easy to make contact, and one day, we invited a young couple back to Nor Siglar. We did not think they had been on a foreign sailboat before. But they had. Five years ago. It was even from Norway! And believe it or not: Martin knew the skipper's family who was from Sagesund where he grew up!

Akberet and Ermias were engaged to be married as soon as the peace treaty with Ethiopia was signed. Both had fought in the war. We will never forget Akberet, who, at only 15 years of age, was sent out to defend her border. "Did you have to kill anybody?" we asked. "Offff courrrrse!" she exclaimed, her lovely hazel eyes flashing with indignation. "Otherwise they would have killed me!" Now, Akberet was 25 years old. It was hard to imagine this stunning woman in army fatigues and wielding a gun. In 1993, the small patriotic population of Eritrea succeeded in defeating and gaining independence from the much bigger Ethiopia. No doubt, it seemed to us, that the feat was due to its exceptionally strong and proud people - especially the women, who must be the most liberated in all of Africa.

We couldn't think of a better place to donate the things we didn't need any more now that our voyage is almost over, than in this poor war-torn country. Akberet volunteered to distribute the rest of our eyeglasses. We also gave her some first aid supplies and clothing. Grateful, she invited us home for an Eritrean Coffee Ceremony, an hour-long ritual during which guests converse and watch the traditional preparation. Skillfully, Akberet roasted the green beans in a metal pan with a long handle over a small charcoal burner. Then, she ground the beans by hand, boiled the coffee in a small clay urn and served it piping hot and sweet in tiny cups in three separate servings. A wooden crate nicely decorated with bougainvillea and greens served as a table.

We stayed for dinner as well. It was a hot and spicy meat and vegetable stew served on several layers of injera, a spongy slightly sour pancake made from sorghum. Eating from the same platter, we felt as if we were part of the family. Everyone broke into the section of injera in front of them, tearing off a piece and dipping it into the stew in the centre. Before and after the meal, the youngest girl in the family came around with a washbasin for everyone to rinse their hands.

The family of ten lived in a brick house of two small rooms and a kitchen. At night, some of them slept outside under a mosquito netting. "That's no problem in this climate," the mother said. She didn't know how old she was. Maybe 55, she thought. She looked much older. Still, she was very beautiful. The family was doing better than average. The father had a good salary. A supervisor at the Department of Fisheries, he earned US$100 a month. Akberet was a secretary at a local shrimp farm. She made US$60 per month. Like Solomon and his family, they had lost everything during the war. But now, they were optimistic about the future. Their first priority was a bathroom. "I am afraid our toilet isn't working," Akberet said, embarrassed as she led me behind a big rock on the beach.

During a two-day outing to Asmara, the capital city, Solomon looked after Nor Siglar for us. When we returned our faithful helper, who wanted only US$10 a day for his services, invited us home to meet his wife and son. "Our home is modest," he warned us. "But we are grateful for what we have."

A beautiful Tigrinya woman grinds beans for a traditional coffee ceremony. She gives us the only decoration she owns right off the wall of her one-room hut.

His home was nothing but a shack with a tin roof, corrugated walls and a dirt floor. It was situated on a hill above a cluster of similar dwellings. "There is more breeze up here," Solomon explained. "Not so many mosquitoes. And we even have a view of the harbour! So we are really quite fortunate," he said. "Brick houses are too warm in this climate," he continued. "Besides," he joked, "you can make your own air conditioning by poking holes in metal walls!"

It was clean and tidy in the one-room hut where the family had all their worldly belongings: a wooden table stacked full of kitchen utensils; sacks of sugar and flour, with cans of cooking oil and kerosene neatly organized below. The walls were decorated with magazine clippings of soccer stars and sailboats, a handmade wall hanging, a blackboard for home schooling and a picture of a black Christ. Clothes hung neatly spaced on nails on the walls. "I have made our bed myself," Solomon said. He had used iron bars for the frame. The mattress was tightly braided from a strong nylon twine. "I have made this basin for drinking water too. It is fibreglass. An American sailor helped me." They had no electricity, no running water and no toilet. Their sanitation facilities were an outdoor communal affair located on the outskirts of the settlement.

Despite such incredible poverty, they treated us to a coffee ceremony. And it was a true delight to see Solomon's 19-year old wife perform the whole ritual, sitting erect as could be on a tiny stool while at the same time breastfeeding their 2-year old son, Alexander. Winny was from the Tigrinya tribe. She was exceptionally beautiful, her hair tightly braided from forehead to crown where it cascaded out over her shoulders like a fan. Her bright white teeth sparkled when she smiled. And that was often.

As we were ready to leave, Winny took down the wall hanging, dusted it off and handed it to us. "For you," she said with a shy smile. "She has made it herself," Solomon explained. "We wish to thank you for everything you have done for us. I wish we had something nicer to give you. But this is all we have to offer." It blew us away. These people had nothing. Still, they had something to share.

Eritrea is the poorest country we have seen. It couldn't possibly be worse. Or so we thought.

DESTITUTE SUDAN

We took our time along Sudan's desolate coast exploring its many khors and marsas – calm, safe anchorages that are accessed via narrow gaps in the coral reefs that run parallel with the shoreline. Some khors are at the end of inlets that wind their way for miles into the desert. About a daysail apart, they offer perfect shelter to exhausted sailors.

In Marsa Sheikh Ibrahim, our very first marsa, we also had our very first encounter with the Sudanese people. We hesitated to go ashore in a land reputed to be a haven for Muslim fundamentalists, and for harbouring and training terrorists. So we were not at all certain how we would be received. But as we have experienced before in places of unsafe reputation, we were met with only kindness.

"Salam' alaykum!" we called to two men on the beach as we were rowing ashore. They looked up, dropped what they were doing and came running down to meet us. "Wa alaykum as-salam!" they greeted, helping us with the dinghy. Their body language indicated that we were welcome. Our few words in Arabic appeared sufficient to create a feeling of goodwill. With the help of finger language and a bit of English, we actually managed to communicate a little.

The men, who were boiling tar in a rusty oil barrel, had three horizontal scars on their cheeks. In Sudan, tribal origin is still identified by facial marks. They were about to put a coat of tar on the bottom of their wooden boats. Pointing to a truck nearby, they seemed to imply that the boats were going to be transported overland. The fishermen were nomads! They were moving from fishing ground to fishing ground by truck! In an attempt to combat espionage and smuggling caused by border conflicts and strife, nearly all inshore traffic has been eliminated in the Red Sea. Consequently, there is hardly any local traffic along the sparsely populated coast. The result is an exceptionally diverse and colourful underwater flora and fauna. And we were among the privileged few to be able to enjoy it.

"Salam' alaykum!" Nomade fishermen greet us warmly in a land where we hesitated to go ashore unsure whether we were safe or even welcome.

We thought Eritrea was poor. But Sudan was even poorer. The fishermen lived in tiny hovels put together with whatever they could find: bits of cardboard, burlap and wooden crates, plastic tarps, twigs and twine. Still, they were unbelievably generous, offering us coffee and giving us the largest, most beautiful shells in their pile. The men seemed pleased with the cigarettes, matches and engine oil that we gave them.

Entering the port of Sawakin, the last slave trading post in the world, was a most dramatic experience. Winding our way for two miles through a narrow channel that brought us within a hundred feet of the crumbling ruins of the once important trading centre, we ended up in a large landlocked basin overlooking the spooky ghost town, where slaves were traded until the end of WWII. A new town had sprung up a little further inland. The atmosphere reminded us of scenes from the film, "Lawrence of Arabia"; the most dominant feature being tall and dashing macho men in turbans and flowing jalabiyyas sporting long silver coated swords or intricately decorated curved daggers. Less visible were the women; tall and lean, enveloped in colourful tobes, a 9-metre piece of cloth, which they also used as camouflage and protection against the desert dust. The market was a virtual Wild West and likely just as lively today as it was way back when. Most chaotic was the noisy and smelly animal market where men were bartering and trading dromedaries and donkeys, chickens and goats.

What a life! For once, we had the opportunity to taste both camel meat and milk. But as the meat market was not very appetizing, we played it safe and stuck with familiar fruits, vegetables and pita bread. Watching the commotion, we felt a thousand eyes upon us. Clearly, people were not used to seeing Caucasians.

At night, the decaying coral buildings of Old Sawakin were bathed in a shroud of darkness. It was eerily quiet too. No music, no noise, not even the monotonous chant of the muezzin. There was no electricity in that part of town. In the daytime, it was busy in the harbour. Busloads of people from all over Sudan came to take the ferry across the Red Sea to Saudi Arabia to participate in the annual pilgrimage to Mecca, not far from Jeddah. Incidentally, our agent, who checked us in and looked after the formalities, was very helpful. Forgetting for a moment that Islam forbids alcohol, we offered him a beer. His face lit up. But we had to go down below where no one could see him drink it.

We needed propane and had to go to Port Sudan to get the container refilled. At the bus station, three little boys were running around selling biscuits, chewing gum and Kleenex. They were real charmers and we bought something from them all. Delighted, they gestured that we should take their picture. We thought it was a trick to make more money. Not at all. Considering how poor they were, we were surprised that they didn't beg.

The bus was packed so we had an excellent opportunity to get close to the passengers. Literally! A man behind us spoke some English. He had "only" two wives and six children. His father had four wives and 26 children. "I am too poor for that," he said. "Besides," he added with a twinkle in his eye: "many wives - many problems!"

On the bus to Port Sudan. "Many wives – many problems," a man explains on the topic of Muslim men having four wives.

The bus trip allowed us a glimpse into the real Africa. The images are imprinted on our minds forever. Especially the never-ending drab and desolate landscape dotted with Bedouins on eternal wanderings with their caravans. What a tough existence these hardy desert nomads lead as they move with their herds from pasture to pasture and tent camp to tent camp, always in search of food for their animals. The women were a haunting sight as they wandered along the road loaded down with bundles of firewood, jugs of water and life's many necessities.

As expected, the northerly winds grew stronger and more constant the further north we went. A group of sailors ahead of us were weather-bound for ten days in an isolated marsa in Egypt, where the military would not allow them ashore. Fortunately, we were never holed up for more than four days at a time. The delays were far from boring. In Marsa Amid, we anchored close to a rundown desalination plant. The guard, who was two metres tall and very black, sat, doubled over for hours on end in the shade of his lean-to overlooking the bay. What was he thinking all day, we wondered? What did he think of the modern boats in the middle of his domain? We would have given anything to read his mind.

On a walk along the dykes and salt flats, we ran into some men at a maintenance yard. They had converted a container, which had washed ashore, into a shelter by cutting openings for windows and doors. Inside were a couple of bunks, a table made from a crate and some ancient cooking utensils. A well-worn prayer mat lay on the floor. "Kaffee?" The man pointed at a soot-covered pot. "Shukran! Shukran!" we replied in our best Arabic. But they were short of water. The fellow disappeared and returned with a juicy watermelon instead.

Two of the men were Christian, two were Muslim. The older Muslim had a dark spot on his forehead, a visible sign of having touched the ground in prayer five times a day throughout his life. "Haj," the younger Muslim declared, nodding respectfully at the older man. He looked very poor. However, as his title and the white crocheted cap he was wearing indicated, he had successfully completed his required pilgrimage to Mecca, and was therefore highly respected by his fellow Muslims.

What is the tall and handsome watchman thinking all day as he stands guard by his shack overlooking the bay?

Sudan is the largest, but one of the least developed plagued by civil war, drought and famine. Even so, everyone we met during our 2-week visit exuded a certain dignity and pride.

In order to make some headway, we tried to do an overnighter. It became an uphill battle. The winds grew more and more fierce as night progressed. Seas became confused. Before long, we were hammered by waves, which soaked us to the bone. Soon, a thick layer of salt covered Nor Siglar. The sheets became stiff and awkward to handle. Conditions were atrocious. We had never experienced anything like it. After 20 hours of bucking into the rough seas, tacking and beating hard on the wind, we could only record 40 nautical miles. "A night to remember," Martin noted in the log when the nightmare was over. "A night to forget," I countered, bone-tired.

We soon learned that if a fresh breeze were already blowing at sunrise, we would have a full gale by ten. So the best tactic was to start before daylight and cover as much ground as possible before the wind piped up. This way, we could get safely behind the reef and anchor early while the sun was still high in the sky and the visibility good. The charts were poor and rarely corresponded with the GPS, so we had to keep a good lookout to be able to estimate the depth from the colour of the water. We learned to note our GPS-positions on the way in, so that we could retrace our course on the way out in darkness the next morning.

Sailing north in the Red Sea against strong winds and steep seas in a challenge we shall never forget.

We clawed our way north to Khor Shinab, one of the most spectacular anchorages in the Red Sea. The inlet wound its way like a snake over 20 km into the Nubian Desert, where it opened up into a basin surrounded by hills, sand and rock as far as the eye could see. There was no sign of life except a few egrets and the trails of caravans in the distance. We hiked the ridges, wandering from cairn to cairn in the 35-degree heat. The view of the khor was amazing.

25

Anchored all by herself, Nor Siglar was reflected in the mirror of the calm, crystal clear water. The corals were clearly visible from the 200-metre peak above. The area was rich in fossils from the time the desert was under water. We would have liked to stay a while to explore. But the British aircraft carrier, Illustrious, which was participating in an exercise nearby, reported a low in the eastern Mediterranean. That meant a high in the Red Sea with periods of calm and a wind change to the south. It was a weather window we could not afford to miss. For it was impossible to know how long it would be till the next one.

We lucked out and motor-sailed for 42 hours in calm conditions all the way across the infamous False Bay to Egypt. At 23°30′ N, we crossed the Tropic of Cancer. For the last time, Nor Siglar bid the tropics adieu.

EGYPT - THE LAND OF PHARAOHS

The weather window generated an exodus of boats hoping to make a final dash for Suez. It lasted all of 48 hours. When it blew up again, we decided to seek shelter in Sharm Luli, our first anchorage in Egypt. It was a god-forsaken bay. All we could see ashore were some sinister-looking barracks partially hidden in the sand dunes. Martin's back was bothering him. This was definitely not a place to be stuck for any length of time. We would have to find a more civilized place. Safaga was only 150 nautical miles away. We had to make it there somehow.

Two days later, it calmed down enough that Martin thought his back could stand the overnighter to Safaga. We made great progress during the day. By evening, however, his back was so sore that he couldn't do his watches. To stay awake, I nibbled on cookies, drank buckets of tea and updated the log every hour. Nor Siglar was doing well. At breakfast, we only had 15 miles to go. But these turned into a nightmare. Suddenly, the wind veered to the north. In no time, we were blasted by 35- knot winds and 3-metre waves. Other boats turned back. But we were determined to make it. We knew Nor Siglar could do it. She excels in headwinds. We couldn't help but think of the misconception that sailing around the world is a downwind run. It simply isn't the case!

Fortunately, Martin managed to get on his feet to navigate us safely into the harbour. For I couldn't leave the helm for a minute in such treacherous and poorly charted waters. It took us seven hours to do the last 15 miles! But we made it. "Al-hamdu lillah!" Thanks to Allah – and to Nor Siglar!

It was incredibly windy in the anchorage. We worried about dragging and going aground. Kind cruisers helped us put down a second anchor. They also helped us bring jerry cans of water and diesel from the shore. We got soaking wet and cold on the rough dinghy rides. Frequent sandstorms covered the boats in dust. Even though we kept the hatches closed, the fine sand still found its way down below. The solar panels had to be washed every day. Otherwise, they didn't produce enough energy.

Mosque near Port Said.

Martin's condition reminded us of the time 3.5 years ago when he ended up having a back operation in Morocco. At that time, his doctor urged him to quit sailing. Since then, we have almost sailed around the world! Now he was totally immobile again. If we could only make it to Israel! Lying helpless in a bleak and windswept anchorage in Egypt was very depressing. It was hard to see our friends come and go while we had to stay behind.

While Steinar Kopperud from Maria Two kept Martin company and looked after our boats, his wife, Birgitta and I took a trip to Luxor and the Valley of the Kings where we were overwhelmed by fabulous treasures, temples and tombs from Egypt's glorious past. The burial chambers of the pharaohs were exquisitely decorated with hieroglyphics and fresco paintings. Tut Ank Ahmon's tomb contained valuable art and everyday items. His coffin was pure gold. It was astonishing to experience the dramatic contrast between the life we imagined in the temples millennia ago and that of the people living in the region today.

Back on Nor Siglar, Martin's back showed no improvement. I found an internet-café and contacted my brother Knut, who is an orthopaedic surgeon. "You just have to take your time and hope for the best," he said. "There is not much else you can do." Although he didn't have a miracle cure to offer, his moral support was comforting. So I made many trips to the café. Unfortunately, it was also a popular shisha joint frequented by the local men. Puffing away on their gurgling water pipes, they clearly enjoyed watching female tourists sending their emails to distant lands. It was not very pleasant to feel their piercing eyes on my back. In fact, Safaga was the only place on our travels where I felt harassed; especially walking down the street alone. And that was often while Martin was sick. Therefore, Safaga is one of the few places in the world that I really dislike. So when I lost a filling one day, there was no way I would go to a dentist there. Martin made me a temporary filling, which we hoped would last till Israel. What a pathetic pair we were! We couldn't really complain, though. For we have been quite healthy throughout the trip. Apart from our bad backs, of course, and a few cuts and bruises every now and then.

The doctor was right. After a 3-week rest, Martin was well enough to continue. The timing coincided with the arrival of our friends Shayne Dunlop and Gail Davies, who came to sail with us to Israel. Together, we set out for Suez, 200 nautical miles to the north. But this stretch, where the Red Sea narrows into the the Gulf of Suez, is considered to be the toughest part of the inland sea, offering a whole range of challenges: abandoned, unlit oil rigs cut off at sea level, unmarked reefs, large fishing fleets conducting unpredictable manoeuvres and, of course, fierce headwinds. Despite the busy traffic in the Strait of Gubal, we crossed the shipping lane and made our way through a maze of oil platforms marked by flickering flames, to the Sinai Peninsula, where the wind was supposed to be weaker. It had taken us four days to get this far. Now, we wanted to reach Suez at any cost and ran the engine at full speed. In the strong headwinds and steep seas, it burned much more fuel than usual. So when we only had ten miles to go, we ran out of diesel! We couldn't believe it. What next? A fellow sailor appeared out of nowhere and gave us a couple of cans.

Our challenges were not finished yet. For as we were about to enter the Suez Canal Yacht Club, we were clobbered by a khamsin – a terrific sandstorm packing 50-knot winds. So we had quite a struggle before we could throw our mooring lines to the "Prince of the Red Sea", supposedly the only honest agent in all of Suez. Our Red Sea experience was over.

We only had time to visit the museum in Cairo and to take a camel ride around the Sphinx and the spectacular Pyramids of Ghiza before embarking on the Suez Canal. The canal, which opened in 1869, is 193 km long and 11-12 metres deep. Initially operated by an international company, Egypt took over the administration in 1956. After the Six-day War of 1967, it was closed until 1975. War memorials, military paraphernalia, floating bridges and docks were among the haunting sights of the muddy waterway.

There are no locks in the Suez Canals - so it looks more like a long ditch. The transit, which took two days including a layover on Lake Ismailia, was a real test in patience and fortitude. Our pilot was greedy, aggressive and offensive. "Wife hospital four years!" he blurted out as he came onboard. He was really obnoxious and wouldn't leave Gail and me alone. It was extremely unpleasant. The pilot was more concerned with baksheesh than guiding us to Port Said. He kept harping about the bribe the whole way. Not only for himself, but for the police, customs officers and a variety of other colleagues as well.

The poverty, bureaucracy and finally, the bartering of the Arab world, got to us in the end, so it was heavenly to set out into the Mediterranean back to familiar waters and cultures again.

BACK IN ISRAEL – WE DIT IT!

Israel, May 9: Nor Siglar crossed her own wake from May 31 four years previous. Finally, we could call ourselves circumnavigators! We flew the flags from 76 countries and island nations as we entered Ashkelon Marina, where they recognized us from the East Mediterranean Yacht Rally four years ago. We received a champagne welcome and lots of attention. Even from the media. It is quite an event to complete a circumnavigation in Israel. Another highlight occurred on May 17, Norway's Constitution Day, when we had the

Meeting Shimon Peres at the Norwegian Embassy in Israel.

honour of meeting Shimon Peres at a reception in the Norwegian Embassy. Fortunately, Martin was wearing a jacket and tie for the occasion. Only the second time in nine years!

Nor Siglar was caked with salt and orange grime, her sheets stiff and her sails dirty. After a gigantic cleanup and a visit to the dentist, we moved on to Herzlia Marina a day sail away, where an Israeli friend, Itay Singer, whom we met in Fiji, gave us another royal welcome together with his family and friends. The kindness extended by the Singer family was in sharp contrast to what was happening around us. Israel was in the process of withdrawing its troops from Lebanon, an activity we could both hear and see from the marina, which was located below the flight path of gunship helicopters bringing soldiers home. May 14, Israel's Independence Day, was marred by suicide bomber attacks in Hebron, which caused several deaths. Places we had visited last time were not only unsafe but inaccessible as well. We were fortunate to have seen so much at that time. Security was strict everywhere. At the post office, we had to show proof of ID to send a package. Guards posted outside buildings and malls performed full body checks. In Israel, they are more interested in searching people's bags, briefcases and backpacks before they enter the shops than after!

"There is no point giving Arafat a finger," our friend, Itay declared. "He will take the whole hand! He simply doesn't want us here." As we were ready to leave, he gathered a group of friends at their favourite restaurant in Tel Aviv for a send-off party. The mostly Jewish clientele and Palestinian staff seemed to get along well. They were laughing, joking and teasing one another. Little did they know that the area would be haunted by suicide bombers in the very near future. For the negotiations between Israel and Palestine at Camp David were going nowhere. And with the announcement of an independent Palestinian state in September, the conflict was about to escalate and reach catastrophic proportions.

Martin's back was still giving him trouble. For a while, it didn't look like we would be able to continue. But after a few weeks of R&R and VIP treatment in the luxurious marina, he felt better. We decided to give it a try. We were two weeks behind schedule and had to keep at it if we were going to make it across the Bay of Biscay and the North Sea before the autumn storms set in. Our journey through the Mediterranean had to be more like a delivery trip than a cruise, with only short stops for bunkering and re-provisioning. That was fine with us. For we had sailed the Mediterranean twice before.

The first leg turned into a bit of a surprise. We had expected a relatively easy 3-4 day passage to Crete. But we didn't end up there at all! Gale force headwinds and short steep seas so typical for the Mediterranean forced us to do a lot of tacking. One day, our course took us to Libya in the south; the next day to the Peloponnesian Peninsula in the north. It was a real slog. In the end, we gave Crete a miss and carried on to Malta instead. The "short" 3-4 day trip turned into a 12-day non-stop passage of 1,100 nautical miles! So the Indian Ocean wasn't our last longer crossing after all!

The inner basin of Valetta, Malta's impressive harbour.

In Valetta, Malta's impressive fortress city, we only took time to shop for fresh food, fill diesel and water. In fact, we were so anxious to get going that we simply forgot to check out! It was the first time that happened on the whole trip! It is the norm all over the world to clear in and out on arrival and departure. We were already well on our way to Sicily when Valletta Port Control called us back. We were tempted to ignore the order. However, it was too risky and we turned back. And that was a good thing. If we had continued and been caught, we would have received a fine of US$2,000. Besides, the police were looking for three heroin smugglers from Libya who had escaped from a local prison the night before. So Nor Siglar was thoroughly searched before she was allowed to resume her voyage to Sicily, where we had to seek refuge from a storm approaching from the Balearics further west.

The Mediterranean is known for its "feast or famine" conditions, i.e. too much or too little wind. This time, we experienced mostly calm weather. But since Martin's back was still bothering him, we didn't mind. Under the circumstances, we were better off running the engine in calm weather than battling a gale on the nose. Our faithful "Mr. Perkins" purred like a cat for six days in a row all the way to Formentera, where we stopped for fuel. And the engine kept it up for four more days until we reached Gibraltar, where we arrived safely exactly one month after leaving Israel.

Only 1,800 nautical miles to go! What a relief! Our joy was short-lived. While ashore changing money, an unwanted guest had snuck aboard. We found him hiding in the forepeak. We caught him off-guard and the thief had not had time to steal anything. What he did manage, however, was to ruin our evening. Instead of celebrating the halfway point of our last leg with a nice dinner out, we ended up at a police station under the famed "Rock" delivering a report until the wee hours.

It only takes an hour by air from Gibraltar to Casablanca, so we treated ourselves to a quick visit to "our family" in Mohammedia who were so kind to us when Martin had his back operation. We stuffed our backpacks full of clothes and things we knew they could use, and that we didn't need any more now that we were going home. It was an emotional reunion and we had many heart-warming moments together. Our Muslim friends still mean a lot to us. The two little boys are like our grandchildren now. In a way we have "adopted" them.

Back in Gibraltar, we realized that we didn't have any charts to get us to Norway. We had sold them! When we left Halden six years earlier, the idea had been to sail back to Vancouver. We had not intended to return. However, plans change. Our cruise kept expanding and now we were back. In order to avoid a third Atlantic crossing, we had decided to end our odyssey in Norway. A fellow sailor kindly lent us the charts we needed. We were ready for the homestretch.

HOMEWARD BOUND
GIBRALTAR – NORWAY

We had been worrying about the exposed coast of Portugal with its strong prevailing northerly winds. Our rough journey south, in a following gale and high seas was still vivid in our minds. Martin's back was still sore and we were grateful to Pieter Jongeneel for coming to give us a hand again. This time, however, the weather gods were kind and gave us exceptionally favourable conditions.

As Nor Siglar sailed out into the Strait of Gibraltar, hundreds of dolphins came charging after us. Maybe all the bad luck, which we had been experiencing the past year was over? For dolphins mean good luck, and that is exactly what happened. First, we motor sailed on glassy calm seas for three days all the way to Bayona on the north coast of Spain. Then, we had a pleasant crossing of the Bay of Biscay in a fresh breeze from the southwest. It was so stable that we could have all our meals at the cockpit table. Unbelievable but true!

Near the Isles of Scilly, we crossed our old course from the Azores to Norway. That time, we had sailed up the English Channel. It was an experience we did not care to repeat. This year, having made such excellent progress, we had time to take the Irish Sea and the Caledonia Canal instead, a route we had enjoyed on our way south four years ago.

In Howth Marina north of Dublin, a young Norwegian couple recognized us from our articles in the sailing magazine, Seilas. They had just completed the first month of their blue water cruise. It was touching to see them filled with excitement and expectation in anticipation of the biggest adventure of their lives. We were nearing the end of ours. Saturated by impressions and events, we willingly shared our experiences and ideas.

Some of the nicest memories from our circumnavigation were created by these surprise encounters. It was so exciting to hear: "Wow! Isn't that Nor Siglar?" All over the world, we met sailors who had read our articles. "Anne and Martin! Thanks to your inspiration we are embarking on our dream!" a countryman called in passing, as he was heading south to warmer climes.

Our journey continued through the Crinan Canal, a neat "do-it-yourself" experience where we operated eight manual locks on a narrow 18 km canal, which meandered through a peaceful and pastoral countryside. The Caledonia Canal took much longer. It was 100 km long with 29 serviced locks and ten swing bridges. We spent five days on this beautiful waterway, winding our way through the Scottish Highlands past Mt. Nevis and across lakes and lochs where we scouted in vain for the legendary Loch Ness monster.

Even before leaving Gibraltar, we started receiving e-mails indicating that preparations were underway to celebrate our arrival. It was, of course, nice that people wanted to make a fuss over us. However, that meant having to give them an exact time of arrival well ahead. And that was difficult. Deadlines and itineraries were some of the things we had learned to leave behind us. However, all went according to plan. Our good luck was holding and the homestretch went beyond expectations. Even the North Sea was benign.

We easily met the deadline. In strong winds and overcast skies, 15 sailboats from the Halden Yacht Club met us at the famous bridge on the border between Norway and Sweden to escort us the last few miles to the King's Quay. Images from our landfall seven years ago flashed through our minds. Again, a large crowd had turned out to welcome us.

But the only person I saw was my mother. Now, 95 years old, she had followed us on a map above her bed throughout our voyage. No wonder she was the one to receive the most attention from the media who had arrived to record the event. It was not every day circumnavigators came home to Halden. There were lots of well-wishers and speeches, which culminated in the Halden Yacht Club awarding us a life membership. It was a touching and thoughtful moment.

There was no end to the attention. For me, however, most important of all was that my mother was still with us and able to be present after all these years. Martin had lost both his parents while we were away. Naturally, my mother was happy to have us safe and sound at home again. So were we. And we were relieved that we didn't have any more mishaps at the end of our voyage.

A big moment: Nor Siglar ends her around-the-world adventure in Norway.

Our long honeymoon was over. But the festivities were not. Two weeks later, we continued up the Oslo Fjord to Steilene Lighthouse, where the Chief Editor of Seilas, Henrich Nissen-Lie, came onboard Nor Siglar with a huge bottle of champagne. Sailors from the Royal Norwegian Yacht Club escorted us the last few miles to Dronningen, the Queen's Quay, where once again, we received a royal welcome. Also meeting us were Michael and Gillian West of Khamsin, neighbours from Spruce Harbour Marina, who had left Vancouver on the same day as we did. They had left Khamsin in Barcelona while they took a trip through Europe by land. Their surprise presence was a heart-warming finale to a big adventure.

"It sure doesn't look like she has sailed around the world!" were some of the comments from the dock. Nor Siglar certainly had. We had logged 56,000 nautical miles – approximately 2.5 times around the world at the equator. Obviously, Martin's diligent maintenance program had paid off.

We had become incredibly fond of Nor Siglar. What a versatile lady! Not only is she a trustworthy offshore vessel that brought us safely from port to port across the big oceans in all kinds of conditions. She was also our home – our one and only home - for 15 years. Now, we are going to give her a well-deserved rest in "the old country" where we will be using her as our floating summer home for years to come. Although we are returning to Vancouver to live, we intend to come back to our dear Nor Siglar and explore some of the most beautiful cruising areas in the world - in our land of birth. We have saved the best for last.

BACK ON TERRA FIRMA

When we set out on our blue water voyage, we had only planned to be away for a few years. We never dreamt that we would be gone so long. But it turned out to be much more than a sailing adventure. It became an enormously educational, rewarding and at times, a rather trying experience. And while we saw many beautiful places, it was the people we met along the way that gave the circumnavigation real meaning.

We also experienced the delight of bonding with fellow cruisers, brushed up on history and language skills and learned about other cultures. We came to know and understand lifestyles completely different from our own and learned that it is possible to live quite happily in a variety of ways in this complex and fascinating world. Now that we are back, it is reassuring to feel that this is where we belong. This is where we want to be. We have never been tempted to settle down on an island in paradise. Family and old friends mean much more to us than endless summer and exotic places.

So what have we learned from our adventure? It has taught us respect for people from different backgrounds, cultures and religions. We feel that we have become more tolerant and understanding. We have discovered an inner strength we didn't know we had. And we have learned to appreciate the small things in life. We witnessed how people from other cultures live more simply than we do. Now, we intend to do the same. It remains to be seen how long this new awareness will linger.

We have also seen with our own eyes how people all over this astonishing globe of ours have the same basic needs. Regardless of racial origin, culture, religion and environment, everyone needs air, water and food, shelter, clothing and last, but not least, Love. And all parents wish a better life for their children.

When we follow the news around the world nowadays, we feel more engaged than before somehow. Events far away seem more real now that we have been to so many of the places that make the headlines. Things appear more vivid when we can picture the locations in our minds. Before, they were nothing but a distant name on the map. We can better visualize conditions in conflict areas. And our thoughts go to the people we met there. Images come to mind. One thing remains a mystery for us, though: why is there so much misery in this world where we have met so much kindness?

Now that our circumnavigation is over, we are left with many different feelings. First, there is a sense of relief; a relief that we made it home safely. At the same time, we feel a certain vacuum. A very special lifestyle is over. We feel a bit restless, a bit lost. The future is like an open book. But we anticipate new challenges. An exciting part of the cruising lifestyle is that you discover new qualities about yourself. So now, we would like to explore some of those dormant qualities. We will embark on other projects and adventures. It is time for a change. We look forward to life on terra firma again.

Above all, it is nice to come home and feel that East and West, Home is Best. Still, the Dream will be with us forever.

Anne E. Brevig

APPENDIX 1

FACTS

A summary of the demographics, geography, communications, government, economy etc. of countries and island nations mentioned in this book, based on the World Factbook, 2013 edition.

FACTS – OMAN

FACTS – YEMEN

FACTS – ERITREA

FACTS – SUDAN

FACTS - EGYPT

FACTS - OMAN

Coordinates:	21°00´ N, 57°00´ E
Location:	Middle East, bordering the Arabian Sea, Gulf of Oman and Persian Gulf between Yemen and UAE
Government:	Monarchy
Area:	309,500 sq. km
Coastline:	2,092 km
Population:	3,154,134 (incl. 577,293 non-nationals) (2013) Arab, South Asian (Baluchi, Indian, Pakistani, Sri Lankan, Bangladeshi), African
Capital:	Muscat
Languages:	Arabic (official), English, Baluchi, Urdu, Indian dialects
Religions:	Ibadhi Muslim 75%, other (includes Sunni and Shi'a Muslim, Hindu) 25%
Currency:	Omani rials (OMR)
Industries:	Crude oil production and refining, natural gas and liquefied natural gas production, construction, cement, copper, steel, chemicals, optic fiber
Agriculture:	Dates, limes, bananas, alfalfa, vegetables, camels, cattle, fish
Exports:	Petroleum, re-exports, fish, metals, textiles

FACTS - YEMEN

Coordinates:	15°00´ N, 48°00´ E
Location:	Middle East; borders the Arabian Sea, Gulf of Aden and Red Sea between Oman and Saudi Arabia
Government:	Republic
Area:	527,968 sq. km
Coastline:	1,906 km
Population:	25,408,288 (2013) Mostly Arab; also Afro-Arab, South Asians, Europeans
Capital:	Sanaa
Languages:	Arabic (official)
Religions:	Muslim, some Jewish, Christian and Hindu
Currency:	Yemeni rials (YER)
Industries:	Crude oil production and petroleum refining, small scale production of cotton textiles and leather goods, food processing, handicrafts, small aluminum production factory, cement, commercial ship repair, natural gas production
Agriculture:	Grain, fruits, vegetables, qat, coffee, cotton, dairy products, livestock (sheep, goats, cattle, camels), poultry, fish
Exports:	Crude oil, coffee, dried and salted fish, liquefied natural gas

FACTS – ERITREA

Coordinates: 15°00′ N, 39°00′ E

Location: Eastern Africa; borders Ethiopia and the Red Sea between Djibouti and Sudan

Government: Transitional government

Area: 117,600 sq. km

Coastline: 2,234 km

Population: 6,233,682 (2013) Tigrinya 55%, Tigre 30%, other ethnic groups 15%

Capital: Asmara

Languages: Tigrinya, Arabic and English (official), other ethnic languages

Religions: Muslim, Coptic Christian, Roman Catholic, Protestant

Currency: Nakfa (ERN)

Industries: Food processing, beverages, clothing, textiles, light manufacturing, salt, cement

Agriculture: Sorghum, lentils, vegetables, corn, cotton, tobacco, sisal, livestock, goats, fish

Exports: Livestock, sorghum, textiles, food, small manufactures

FACTS – SUDAN

Coordinates:	15 °00′ N, 30 °00′ E
Location:	North-eastern Africa; borders Libya, Chad, C.A.R., South Sudan, Ethiopia and the Red Sea between Egypt and Eritrea
Government:	Federal republic bordering on authoritarian regime
Area:	1,861,486 sq. km
Coastline:	853 km
Population:	34,847,910 (2013) includes population of South Sudan Sudanese Arab 70%, Fur, Beja, Nuba, Fallata, other 30%
Capital:	Khartoum
Languages:	Arabic (official), tribal dialects, English
Religions:	Sunni Muslim 70%, indigenous beliefs 25%, Christian 5%
Currency:	Sudanese pounds (SDG)
Industries:	Oil, cotton ginning, textiles, cement, edible oils, sugar, soap distilling, shoes, petroleum refining, pharmaceuticals, armaments, automobile/light truck assembly
Agriculture:	Cotton, peanuts, sorghum, millet, wheat, gum arabic, sugarcane, cassava (tapioca), mangoes, papaya, bananas, sweet potatoes, sesame, sheep and other livestock
Exports:	Gold, oil and petroleum products, cotton, sesame, livestock, peanuts, gum arabic, sugar

FACTS – EGYPT

Coordinates:	27° 00´ N, 30° 00´ E
Location:	Northern Africa; borders the Mediterranean Sea between Libya and the Gaza Strip, and the Red Sea north of Sudan and includes the Asian Sinai Peninsula
Government:	Republic
Area:	1,001,450 sq. km
Coastline:	2,450 km
Population:	85,294,388 (2013) Egyptian 99%, other 1%
Capital:	Cairo
Languages:	Arabic (official), English and French (educated classes)
Religions:	Muslim (mostly Sunni) 90%, Coptic Christian 9%, other 1%
Currency:	Egyptian pound (EGP)
Industries:	Textiles, food processing, tourism, chemicals, pharmaceuticals, hydrocarbons, construction, cement, metals, light manufactures
Agriculture:	Cotton, rice, corn, wheat, beans, fruits, vegetables, cattle, water buffalo, sheep, goats
Exports:	Crude oil and petroleum products, cotton, textiles, metal products, chemicals, processed food

THE ROUTE

During her nine years at sea, Nor Siglar logged 56,000 nautical miles (a distance equalling 2,5 times around the world), visiting 47 countries and 29 island colonies on the way.

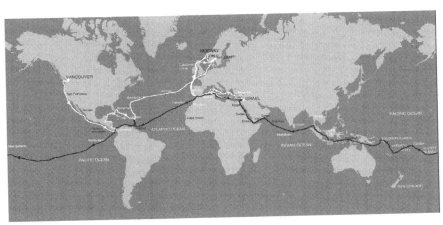

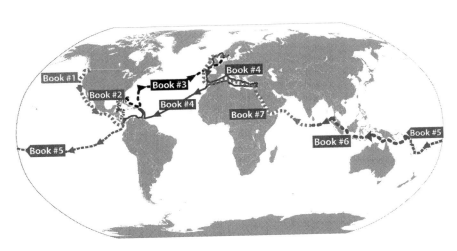

Our sailing route during the 9 Years on the 7 Seas adventure, related to what is covered in each of the 7 books in the Seven Seas Adventures Series.

On the oval map, the "9 Years on the 7 Seas" Route is divided into seven parts, each corresponding to the areas covered in the seven books in the "Seven Seas Adventures" Series.

Anne E. Brevig

APPENDIX 2

MORE ADVENTURES ON THE SEVEN SEAS

Book # 1: **The Dream, the Plan and the Bluewater Debut.**
From Vancouver to the Panama Canal.

Book # 2 **Exploring the East Coast of Central America**
In the Wake of the Pirates of the Caribbean from
Panama to Cuba.

Book # 3: **The Atlantic Crossing Challenge**
On our own Keel from Sunny Caribbean to Wintering
aboard in Norway

Book # 4: **South to warmer Climes**
From the North Sea to the Mediterranean and back
across the Atlantic to the Caribbean.

Book # 5 : **The South Pacific - the Sea of Dreams**
Panama-Galapagos-French,Polynesia-Tonga-Fiji-
Vanuatu-Solomon Islands

Book # 6: **Our South-East Asia Adventures**
Highs and Lows of our Voyage from Australia to the
Maldives.

Book # 7: **The book you are reading now.**

Additional **A Circumnavigator's FAQ**

Information How we Planned, Executed and Survived our
Around-the-World Adventure.

MORE ADVENTURES ON THE SEVEN SEAS

If you have a computer with access to the Internet, you can read this part of the "Seven Seas Adventures" Series as a "Flip-book", based on the illustrated print version of "9 Years on the 7 Seas". **www.sevenseasadventure.com/wedidit** A Flash plug-in is required)

The Series is available in print as well as eBooks in many formats.

The books in the Seven Seas Adventures Series are not just any old travelogues for adventurers. Rather, it is a collection of highlights from encounters with "ordinary" people from different cultures and backgrounds who live a life much different from what most of us are used to. Anne and Martin certainly learned that what we take for granted is an elusive dream for others.

The books "answer" a multitude of questions posed by travellers in general as well as prospective offshore sailors:

Read - and be inspired by how Martin, head of one of the largest forestry consulting firms in Canada and Anne, comptroller of a large shipping company, cut the ties and left their secure jobs and comfortable lives ashore to follow their dreams. Nine years and more than 56,000 nautical miles later, they had survived serious dangers, break-ins and a dramatic grounding, escaped close encounters with pirates, witnessed life-saving bravery and enjoyed heart-warming personal meetings on all five continents.

Get additional reviews and background information, browse image galleries and slideshow presentations, listen to interviews with the author (audio files), read updates and get optional downloads and much more on the Seven Seas Adventures home –

www.sevenseasadventure.com

Book #1: The Dream, the Plan and the Bluewater Debut.

From Vancouver through the Panama Canal

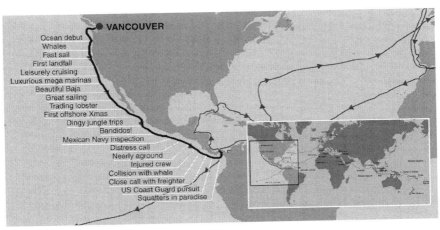

ISBN-13: 978-1494313449
ISBN-10: 1494313448

We start out by sharing last minute hectic preparations and panic before cutting the ties with jobs, home, friends and family and setting out on our "once in a lifetime" adventure.

Come with us on our very first weeklong non-stop ocean passage from Vancouver to San Francisco, feel the "highs & lows" onboard a small craft at sea complete with night watches and seasickness and the exhilaration of making land fall. Explore the fabulous California Coast and sample some of the chores and routines onboard a small sailboat on the wide-open ocean. Experience the logistics of offshore cruising as we meander down the fascinating west coast of Mexico where we have our first encounters with the many challenges involved in our new and "carefree" lifestyle - some anticipated, some not.

It is an adventure where no two days are alike, an adventure about trading fresh lobster for next to nothing in idyllic Bahia Santa Maria and sipping Margaritas in Cabo San Lucas wiggling our toes in the sand; about the beautiful azure blue Sea of Cortes, snorkelling among colourful tropical fishes on spectacular choral reefs, spooky dinghy river trips in the Central American jungle and exploring the Sierra Madre Highlands on primitive "chicken buses", about serenading the Mexican Navy and celebrating Xmas in Puerto Vallarta with cruisers from all over the world.

It is about patrol boats and guns, scary "bandidos" and "friendly inspections", a close call with a freighter and seeing the U.S. Navy in action, chilling distress calls on the ham radio, rough weather in the Gulf of Papagallo, accidental jibes and injured crew, helpful natives, rickety docks and squalls in the night. But it is also about enchanting encounters, trading with natives and visiting a remote Indian village deep in the Panamanian jungle.

Meet an old bohemian couple living their dream on a precious, tropical island in Las Perlas, share with us a rendez-vous with the past, discover dangerous creatures of the sea, witness incredible poverty and crime and come with us through the Panama Canal. There is so much to see, so much to experience. We learn to slow down and smell the roses from squatters on beautiful Isla Paradita who ask: "Why are you rushing through Paradise?"

Book #2: Exploring the East Coast of Central America.

In the Wake of the Pirates of the Caribbean from Panama to Cuba.

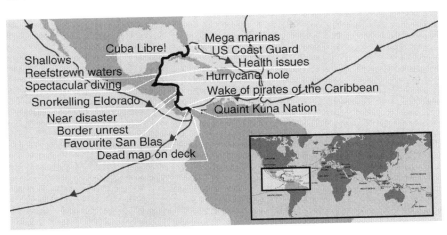

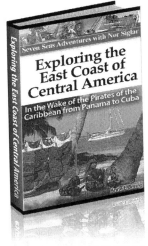

ISBN-13: 978-1494313548
ISBN-10: 1494313545

On our way from Panama to Cuba we sail the historic Spanish Main, once patrolled by the famous pirates and buccaneers, Sir Francis Drake and Henry Morgan in search of the precious Inca gold. We visit the unique islands of San Blas, realm of the Kuna Indians, where we purchase exquisitely hand crafted Molas in exchange for seeing a dead man in a hammock, whom we end up taking to his funeral, using Nor Siglar as a virtual hearse.

We move on to Colombia's isolated Isla Providencia, remote Vivarillo Cays and treacherous Cayo Media Luna, where we come within inches of disaster. We marvel at the hidden Eldorado of the Bay of Honduras with its beautiful islands of Guanaja, Roatan and Utila before seeking refuge from the hurricane season on Rio Dulce in the midst of the jungle, while exploring the fascinating Highlands of Guatemala, the realm of the Maya Indians.

We raise money for an orphanage and get treatment for stomach ailments and hook worms, deal with a cholera scare and thieves in the night, dental work and missing mail. We travel on packed chicken buses with live turkeys and young mothers nursing babies and admire spectacular lakes and bustling markets with impossible names like Chichicastenango, stay at family hotels and enjoy gourmet meals at bargain basement prices, hear of rapes at gunpoint, robberies, street patrols and money in shoes, crime, pollution and such. We marvel at archaeological wonders in the early morning jungle sunrise and learn about medicine doctors and nature's remedies before heading back to the joy of cruising, wet dinghy rides and a boat full of cockroaches.

Then we are off to the dangerous and shallow reef-strewn waters of Belize, one of the most fantastic diving areas in the world and home to the famous Lighthouse Reef and Jacques Cousteau's Blue Hole, where we snorkel with local free divers, trade and feast on lobster and friendship.

Next it's onwards to the Yucatan Peninsula, Mexico's undisputed tourist Mecca, to finish off this part of the voyage in Castro's very own paradise, Cuba, where a whole different world awaits us complete with rules and regulations, inspections and massive bureaucracy. Yet, we are met with unsurpassed friendliness in the midst of appalling poverty and tragedies. We get acquainted with Cuba Libre, shortages, rationing and Fidel's infamous "Committees for the Defence of the Revolution", before heading across the Strait of Florida to the Land of the Free.

Book #3: The Atlantic Crossing Challenge

On our own Keel from Sunny Caribbean to Wintering aboard in Norway

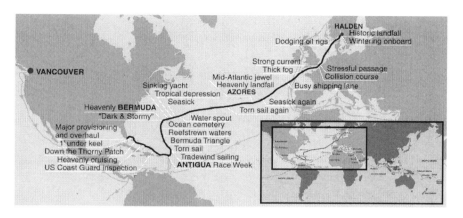

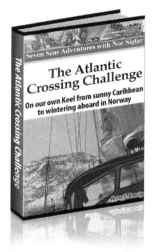

We give Nor Siglar a major overhaul and psyche ourselves up for the Big Atlantic Crossing. But first we do some leisurely cruising in the Bahamas, Turks & Caicos, Dominican Republic, Puerto Rico and the British Virgin Islands before setting out on the first stretch from Antigua to Bermuda. After one week of great trade wind sailing, we find that Bermuda is, as quoted by Mark Twain, "a heavenly place to be but a hell of a place to get to".

Surrounded by treacherous reefs, home to a virtual ocean cemetery, we battle through rough seas for 12 hours to cover the last 20 miles before making heavenly landfall in beautiful and

ISBN-13: 978-1494313562
ISBN-10: 1494313561

sheltered St. Georges Harbour, where the national drink, "Dark and Stormy" awaits weary, but relieved sailors. A virtual botanical garden, world-class golf courses, luxury hotels, pastel coloured English Country style homes with whitewashed roofs designed to collect rainwater into private cisterns, all characterise this tiny 35 km x 1 km island where we enjoy three weeks of R&R before heading out into the Atlantic again for the next leg to the Azores.

With a tropical depression threatening to derail us, we postpone the start by a few days, spooked by sailboats ahead sinking, some crew drowning, some getting rescued at sea. Our own crossing proceeds without major problems apart from the usual seasickness, a scary waterspout and an approaching hurricane, long and lonely night watches and close encounters with freighters on collision course in the black of the night. After two weeks of non-stop sailing, the lush and green island of Faial in the Azores provides us with much needed R&R before the last and longest stretch to Norway. But first, there are repairs and maintenance to be done and a painting from Nor Siglar's crew on the docks of Horta, which is the custom of visiting sailors. No painting means bad luck and who wants that for the next leg of their crossing? It certainly gives us good luck, as with a change of crew, we complete the relatively uneventful leg in three weeks, albeit with considerable struggle through the English Channel, where we battle fog, strong currents and busy shipping lanes, the most stressful challenge of our voyage to date. Reaching the familiar North Sea, we feel we are almost there, but having to dodge a multitude of oilrigs and tack back and forth in stubborn headwinds between the south coast of Norway and the west coast of Denmark, doubles the remaining distance.

Frustrated but happy, we make landfall in Halden, Anne's home town, having reached the first goal of sailing to our "old country" on our own keel all the way from our new country, Canada. So after a memorable Homecoming, we settle down to wintering aboard during the coldest winter Norway has experienced in years!

Book #4: South to warmer Climes

From the North Sea to the Mediterranean and back across the Atlantic to the Caribbean.

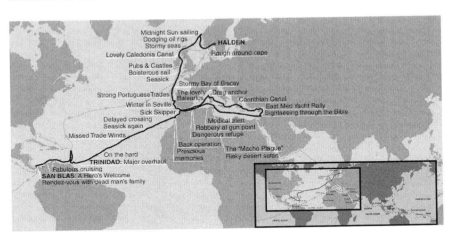

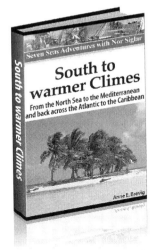

ISBN-13: 978-1494313609
ISBN-10: 149431360X

After an eventful year in Norway, we set course south in search of endless summer, calling first on the barren islands of Shetland and the Orkneys, rich in our Viking heritage and where we meet unsurpassed friendliness. We transit the Caledonia Canal with its pristine lakes scouting in vein for the infamous Loch Ness monster, explore the beautiful Scottish Highlands and head into the Irish Sea to its southern port, Crosshaven, where we visit some of Ireland's famous pubs, castles and the oldest yacht club in the world.

The dreaded Bay of Biscay is before us and we get a boisterous start, a formidable test of sea legs, endurance and resolve. Whose idea was this, anyway? But as always, the scare and discomfort are well worth the effort, and after seven uncomfortable days at sea, we make landfall in Portugal's quaint, old port of Oporto. After a well deserved rest and massive clean-up aboard, we sample the local delicacies; port wine and Vino Verde, sardines and baccalau prepared in a multitude of ways, before continuing in strong Portuguese trade winds down the Iberian Coast calling on charming fishing villages cum resorts. We head up the Guadalquivir River to spend the winter in Carmen's beautiful Seville, brush up on our Spanish and tour Andalucía's many stunning Pueblos Blancos. After the traditional Semana Santa, we continue our journey through the Strait of Gibraltar to the spectacular anchorages of the Balearics, mountainous Corsica, picturesque Sardinia and historic Sicily.

The Mediterranean lives up to its "Feast or Famine" reputation, i.e. either too much or too little wind. We get them all: levanters and mistrals, meltemis and sciroccos, which produce strong and relentless winds with stormy gusts and short, steep seas, which create havoc in anchorages causing many sleepless nights. We hesitate to leave Nor Siglar to see the sights ashore. Still, we manage to get a good sampling of the many ancient ruins of Greece, and Turkey too, where we have our first encounter with the Muslim world and the mysteries of the exotic East. Together with 100 boats, we enter the East Mediterranean Yacht Rally from Antalia to North Cyprus and Israel where we go sightseeing through the Bible and experience first-hand the realities of today. We sail to Malta, and anchored in the middle of war torn Grand Harbour, meet the tough and heroic Maltese.

We continue to Tunisia and take a memorable safari in the desert, sail along off-limits Algeria, where we seek refuge anyway, and are almost robbed at gun point and finally, to Gibraltar to prepare for our Atlantic crossing back to the Caribbean. But on the way to the Canary Islands, misfortune strikes. The skipper suffers a herniated disc, necessitating an emergency stop in Morocco.

After seven painful weeks flat on his back, he has a successful operation in Casablanca. So what started as a depressing situation became a very positive experience as we befriended many locals, and in particular, the family of the night watchman in the Marina, who was extremely kind, bringing us home cooked dinners every night for three months free of charge. We learned a lot about their lifestyle and culture and once again, experience how nice and kind people are all over the world regardless of background, colour, culture and faith.

A month after the operation, we set out across the Atlantic again, and despite a rather rough crossing in nasty gales and scary seas, we reach Trinidad safely in three weeks. With Nor Siglar on the hard for the hurricane season, we take a break to visit family and friends in

Canada and Norway. On our return, she gets a thorough overhaul before we head back to the Western Caribbean and the spectacular reef anchorages of Venezuela and the lovely islands of the Lesser Antilles; Aruba, Bonaire and Curacao. In San Blas, we get a Heroes' Welcome from the Kuna Indians who remember us from six years earlier when we helped them transport a dead man on Nor Siglar's deck to his funeral. The unique rendez-vous gains us carte blanche to sights and activities "ordinary tourists" would never get access to and is a fascinating experience to treasure.

We end this long part of our journey – 18,000 nautical miles over four years - by transiting the Panama Canal for a second time, pointing our bow into the South Pacific for an adventure yet to be determined.

We have been away for seven years. Should we head north and home? Or should we continue southwest to the Paradise of Dreams – the romantic and alluring South Seas? Stay tuned.

Book #5: The South Pacific - the Sea of Dreams

Panama-Galapagos-French,Polynesia-Tonga-Fiji-Vanuatu-Solomon Islands

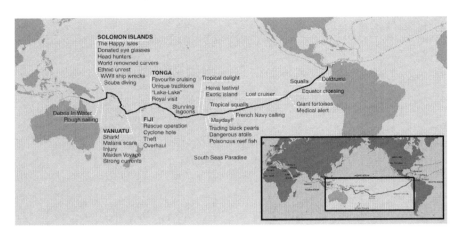

ISBN-13: 978-1494313647
ISBN-10: 1494313642

Gliding out of the last lock in the Panama Canal, we find ourselves at a crossroads. Seven years into our adventure, which was supposed to last 3-4, we should really be heading north and home. But the lure of the South Seas proves too strong, and we set sails in the opposite direction, committing ourselves to several more years at sea.

Experienced and confident, we are ready to tackle the long ocean passages on our own without crew. Another milestone is reached between Panama and Galapagos: We cross the Equator into the southern hemisphere and offer libations to King Neptune. Once on the barren island, we stand face to face with the giant tortoises of Galapagos, meet descendents of Norwegian settlers from the 1920's, learn to deal with corrupt officials, nasty infections and a sore back.

We prepare Nor Siglar and ourselves both mentally and physically for the 3-week crossing to the Marquesas. An uneventful passage in ideal conditions for us, yet another cruiser gets lost, his boat later found in Acapulco with no one onboard. After 3000 nautical miles, we celebrate landfall in rugged and mountainous Hiva Oa, our first introduction to legendary French Polynesia: air laden with the heavy scent of tropical fruit and flowers, beautiful "vahines" with flowers in their hair dancing the erotic hula-hula, macho, tattooed men racing outrigger canoes, gourmet food and joie de vivre.

More awaits us in the beautiful but dangerous Tuamotus Archipelago where we hear a "Mayday" call from a sailboat sinking on a reef. In the little Atoll of Ahe, we trade locally harvested black pearls, collect breadfruit and pample mousse and learn to avoid reef fish, which may cause ciguatera poisoning.

We cruise the magic Society Islands of Tahiti, Moorea and Bora Bora with their stunning turquoise crystal clear lagoons that provide sheltered anchorages behind treacherous reefs and experience their month long Heiva celebration, a cultural festival complete with old, Polynesian competitions and traditional song and dance.

A 10-day brisk sail further west lies the lovely Kingdom of Tonga, where never having been colonized, traditions and culture are strong and we marvel at their unique pandanus basketry and crafts, tapa clothing and special "laka laka" song-play and dance. We feast on pigs roasted on the spit, food wrapped in banana leaves cooked in underground ovens and experience our first kava ceremony. Amazingly, one day Tonga's 300 lb. 80-year old king comes swimming out to Nor Siglar and circles her several times as part of his daily exercise routine.

Four days further west, friendly Fiji beckons with a whole set of new customs and traditions. Here we are addressed as Mr. and Mrs. Martin and here we lose our passports and credits cards and because of this delay, also lose the weather window to continue to Australia. So we spend the cyclone season in Fiji instead, as it is paramount for offshore cruisers to be in the right place at the right time.

We put Nor Siglar on the hard and fly home to visit family and friends. Five months later, we find her exactly as we left her and proceed to give her a thorough overhaul, even a paint job, as the price is right so long as we can stand the slow, built-in "Fiji Factor". A cruiser friend ends up on a reef and we help out in the dramatic rescue operation before setting out to Vanuatu, five days to the west.

We spend three great weeks cruising the islands of Efate, Epi, Ambryn, Pentecost and Espiritu Santu, experiencing everything from bungee land diving and war dances in the buff to building outrigger canoes, helping an injured native and a close encounter with a shark. We learn about Black Magic, coming-of-age rituals and pig killings with clubs, the many taboos, arranged marriages and bride prices and some of their pigeon English language, Bislama, where a helicopter is simply called "mixmaster blongs Jesus" and history is "taem blong befoa".

A rough seven-day crossing to the Solomon Islands tests our nerves and abilities and in a veritable "Mother of all Squalls", thoughts of quitting the adventure start to form in our minds. In Morovo lagoon, known for its fabulous scuba diving on the many ship wrecks from WW2, we meet the world-renowned carvers of the South Pacific, but wonder about their integrity when told that one of them had rescued JFK. We trade with these descendents from the vicious headhunters, donate eyeglasses in a small village and find out how to avoid malaria.

We love the Solomon Islands, the best-kept secret in the Pacific, but it is time to move on with the seasons, and now Australia is calling next.

Book #6: Our South-East Asia Adventures

Highs and Lows of our Voyage from Australia to the Maldives

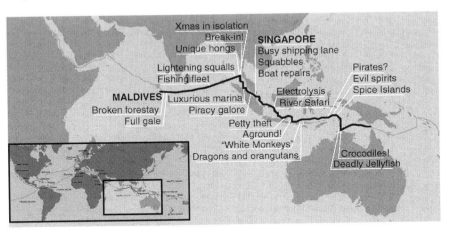

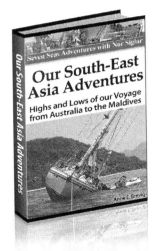

ISBN-13: 978-1494313678
ISBN-10: 1494313677

Our passage in the wake of Captain Bligh across the Coral Sea through the Torres Strait to Gove in Northern Australia is one of the toughest in our eight years of cruising; a close-hauled nightmare bucking into fierce headwinds and rough, breaking seas, dodging nasty rain squalls and heavy traffic through busy shipping lanes.

Avoiding pollution and debris in the water off the coasts of the Louisiades and Papa New Guinea is a new challenge for us. We do the 1,400 nautical miles non-stop in 14 days and savour a ten-day break, somewhat marred by threats of crocodiles, deadly jellyfish and electrolysis, before reprovisioning for two months in Indonesia.

Nervous about piracy in this part of the world, we sail in convoy with six other boats. Our worst scare, however, is overcrowded fishing boats with men in black balaclavas skirting our bows at high speed attempting to get rid of evil spirits onboard, but also their lack of navigation lights at night and petty thefts at anchor off remote villages.

We visit the famed Spice Islands in the Moluccas, bypass unsafe Timor and cruise the southern chain of Nusa Tenggara with its spectacular volcanoes and quaint mountain villages known for their "ikat" weavers, colourful markets, arts and crafts and traditional dances.

We stand face to face with bloodthirsty Komodo dragons, meet our closest cousin, the orang-utan on a 3-day river trip in Kalimantan, visit fishing villages with golden domed mosques and rest up at a peaceful home stay in central Bali surrounded by lush and green terraced rice fields and quaint temples.

We learn about rituals, rites and reality and attend a Hindu cremation in the free.

Near disaster strikes when we go hard aground and almost lose Nor Siglar were it not for fellow cruisers who come to our aid in the 11th hour. More troubles lurks in the South China Sea; the ham radio cuts out and electrolysis is eating up our propeller. But the problems are easily fixed in Singapore's modern Raffles Marina where cruisers debate a sailor's dilemma prompted by having passed a dead man floating in the Java Sea without picking pick him up, concerned about legal and beauracratic ramifications.

We cross the heavily trafficked and infamous pirate infested Strait of Malacca, spend a month in Langkawi, and leave Nor Siglar safely in Rebak Marina while touring Malaysia and Thailand by land, a nice break after five months onboard and almost 6,500 nautical miles since leaving Fiji. On our return we move north to spend Christmas in splendid isolation in Thailand's picturesque Phang Nga Bay and tour a "hong" near James Bond's Paradise Island by dinghy, while thieves break in onboard Nor Siglar. Fed up, we move south to tiny and beautiful Phi Phi Don and ring in the New Year on Patong Beach near Phuket with thousands of other revellers. With the expansive Indian Ocean ahead of us, and not many places to provision on the way, we do a humungous provisioning and set off to the Maldives 2,800 nautical miles to the west. More trouble looms on the horizon as we are plagued with thunder and lightening squalls, fortunately escaping any strikes but the furling forestay suddenly snaps, resulting in frantic manoeuvres on the foredeck. We manage to get hold of it and the situation is saved but our endurance is running thin. "I am getting too old for this", Martin exclaims. But then, when making landfall in tiny Uligamu in the northern Maldives, life is good again. The island is gorgeous, the people pleasant, the culture interesting and who can complain about swimming with manta rays? We feel we have landed in the last paradise on earth.

A Circumnavigator's FAQ

How we Planned, Executed and Survived our Around-the-World Adventure

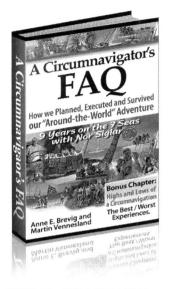

ISBN-13: 978-1494313753
ISBN-10: 1494313758

"Do you have any favourite places?" "Were you ever in danger?" "What would you do differently?" "Were you ever sick?"

These are but a few of the many questions Norwegian-Canadian couple, Anne Brevig and Martin Vennesland were often asked after they had finished their 56,000 nautical mile circumnavigation immortalized in their immensely popular book, "9 Years on the 7 Seas with Nor Siglar".

Time and again, when promoting their bestseller at boat shows, slide shows on-board cruise ships and a multitude of nautical and cultural organizations, people would invariably ask the very same questions. Hence the idea to collect the most frequently answered ones in a handy little FAQ-book. And here it is: "A Circumnavigator's FAQ", a book chock full of information, which will be useful to sailors and discriminating travellers alike, especially to those who yearn to get off the beaten track far away from the traditional tourist routes.

Here you can get straight answers from a couple who sought freedom from the everyday grind by cutting all ties and set sails for the unknown to live their dream and explore life on the other side of the horizon. During their once-in-a-lifetime fabulous, but also challenging adventure, which was filled with drama and excitement, strange and enchanting encounters, heartwarming hospitality and places of breathtaking beauty, they visited 76 countries and island nations covering a distance equaling 2.5 times around the world at equator. So now you are about to read an abbreviated version of the wisdom gained by these two experienced globetrotters who lived 15 years on their 40-foot sailboat, nine of them offshore.

Not only to they share valuable, real-life tips and ideas on how to enjoy the unknown and avoid dangers, but they also offer life-tested advice and recommendations.

One of the most Frequently Asked Questions was: "Do you have one all-important advice to other travelers?"

Read the adventurous couple's answer to this - and many other questions in this book, which cover the topics of Planning, Executing and Surviving a Around-the-World Adventure.

THE HIGHS AND LOWS OF A CIRCUMNAVIGATION

Our best and worst Experiences during our Seven Seas Adventure.

The "Highs"

- Close contact with foreign cultures, especially the primitive ones.
- Crossing the Equator and completing the actual circumnavigation.
- Spectacular sunsets and mile long beaches of California and Mexico
- Panama and Corinthian Canals.
- Paradisiacal anchorages.
- Back alleys.
- Snorkeling among colorful coral fish and spectacular underwater flora.
- Trading with natives, especially the fabulous woodcarvers of Solomon Islands.
- To help poor people in isolated areas with eyeglasses ("Gift of Eye Sight"), first aid and whatever "expertise" we could supply
- The "San Blas experience", where we helped a Kuna Indian family transport a deceased man on Nor Siglar's deck from one island to another.
- Martin's back operation in Morocco, which resulted in the "adoption" of a Muslim family who took such good care of us there.
- The closeness between fellow offshore cruisers.
- Ham radio contacts and the maritime mobile nets.
- Mail parcels from home (pre e-mail era).
- Meeting sailors around the world who recognized us from our articles in the Norwegian sailing magazine, "Seilas".

Favorite Places

- San Blas, Panama
- The Kuna Indian culture and unique experiences. (SSA #2), (SSA #4)
- Honduras and Guatemala
- The Maya Indian culture and interesting experiences. (SSA #2)
- Belize
- Snorkeling in the most fantastic underwater paradise. (SSA #1)
- Turkey
- The friendly Turks, spectacular historic sights and anchorages. (SSA #4)
- Tonga
- The culture, song, music and wonderful anchorages. (SSA#5)
- French Polynesia
- The culture, the beauty of the people, the song, music and joie de vivre, the lagoons, atolls and spectacular anchorages. (SSA #5)
- Vanuatu and Solomon Islands
- The primitive culture, the superb wood carvers and unique experiences. (SSA #5)

In general, the places we enjoyed the most where those where we stayed the longest. Staying in the same place for a longer period of time gives the natives a chance to get used to you. In this way, it is possible to make closer contacts with the locals and to form more personal bonds. This is also how one gets the most unique experiences. We have found this to be the case, particularly in remote islands with primitive culture and lifestyle.

So it is the people we met along the way that made the biggest impression on us, not the nature. There are many gorgeous places in the world. To experience genuine human encounters, however, is rare. Therefore, when we consider which places we'd like to go back to, it is always to those where we made the closest contact with the locals and where we had the most heartwarming experiences.

The "Lows"

- Seasickness.
- Collision with a whale. (SSA #1)
- Injured crew during a gale in the Gulf of Papagayo (Nicaragua). (SSA #1)
- Near grounding/disaster dragging anchor in Honduras (SSA #2) and Greece (SSA #4).
- Seeking refuge and being under 24 hour armed guards surveillance in Algeria. (SSA #5)
- Frequent back problems (both) and the Skipper's disk operation in Morocco. (SSA #5)
- Running aground in Fiji and Indonesia. (SSA #6)
- Break-ins in Thailand and Gibraltar as well as an aborted attempt in Algeria. (SSA #6)
- Electrolysis. (SSA #6)
- Unsafe, war-torn countries. (SSA #7)
- Pirate infested waters. (SSA #7)
- Entangled in a huge commercial fishnet in the middle of the Indian Ocean. (SSA #7)

Dangers

The most dangerous situation we experienced was when we got entangled in a huge fish net in the Indian Ocean (SSA #7). As far as the groundings were concerned; the first one (Fiji – SSA #5) was harmless, while the second one (Indonesia – SSA #6), could have ended in a disaster. But only for Nor Siglar - we could have waded safely ashore!

The break-ins were also harmless. We caught both thieves in the act, so they didn't have time to take anything. Apart from these incidents, we only had two dinghy ropes stolen. The first time, the dinghy was moored in a fishing harbour in Bonifacio (Corsica). The second time was on a remote beach in Vanuatu. In Guatemala (Livingston), we lost a pair of old boat shoes and a pail of garbage which we had left in the cockpit overnight. The outboard engine is the most popular and frequently stolen item of an offshore sailor. Therefore, we decorated it, as well as the dinghy, with brightly coloured drawings, so that they were both easily identifiable. And it worked! Nobody wanted them.

Places we did not like

- Colon and Panama City, Panama
  Theft and crime, violence and poverty. (SSA #2)
- Egypt, The Suez Canal,
  Unprofessional pilots, perpetual begging and bribery, aggressive males. (SSA #7)
- Some Greek Islands
  Too many tourists, aggressive salesmen and charter boats. (SSA #4)
- Most of the Eastern Caribbean Islands.
  Too many tourists, aggressive salesmen and charter boats. (SSA #2) .

Anne E. Brevig

A SHORT SUMMARY OF A 9-YEAR CIRCUMNAVIGATION

It is difficult to make a short summary of a 9-year adventure, however, here goes:

THE ROUTE:

Departure Vancouver 1/9/1991 – through the Panama Canal, April, 1992 - through the western and eastern Caribbean incl. Cuba and the Bahamas, crossing the Atlantic from Antigua to Bermuda, then nonstop from the Azores to Norway, arriving in July, 1993, wintered onboard in Halden during the cold year of the Lillehammer Olympics. Departed Norway, July 1994 for Shetland and the Orkneys, continued through the Caledonian Canal in Scotland to Ireland and south to the Mediterranean where we spent 1-½ years. Then crossed the Atlantic again - back to Trinidad and onwards through the Panama Canal for a second time, March 1998. Crossed the Pacific Ocean via Galapagos, Tuamotus, French Polynesia and Tonga to Fiji, arriving September 1998, where the boat was on the hard in Vuda Point Marina during the cyclone season, ending May, 1999. From there on to Vanuatu, the Solomon Islands, PNG, Australia, Indonesia, Singapore, Malaysia and Thailand (where we spent Christmas and New Year, 2000), crossing the Indian Ocean via the Maldives to Oman, through the Gulf of Aden and up the Red Sea to Israel, where the circumnavigation was first completed but did not end. Thereafter, we went straight through the Mediterranean for a third time and reached Norway via Ireland and the Caledonian Canal, arriving Halden 20/8/2000

DISTANCE, DURATION AND LAYOVERS

During the nine-year circumnavigation, NOR SIGLAR visited 47 countries and 29 island colonies. Total distance logged was ca. 56,000 nautical miles (2.6 times around the world at equator), of which ca. 20,000 nm (35%) were motoring or motor-sailing. The voyage was accomplished in 3285 days. Approximately 3/4 of the time (70%) was spent in port, 15% at sea, and the rest (15%) on land trips and travels home, i.e. we spent 5,5 times as long in harbours and ashore than at sea, as is evident from the following statistics:

At Sea.	Under sail	326 days	65%	
	By motor or motor-sailing:	176 days	35%	
	Total days at sea:	502 days		15%
In Port	Anchorages	316 days		
	Marinas and/or buoys(*)	181 days		
	Total Port Calls	497 days		
	Total Days in Port	2283 days		70%
Trips home by plane		500 days		15%
VOYAGE GRAND TOTAL (9 years)		3285 days		100%

(*) Includes 6 times on the hard (layover in a yard). A good third of the marina stays where in Norway during the one year sojourn there.

OPERATIONS STATISTICS:

1) Engine Hrs	Motor and Motor sailing	4233 hours	(176 days)	82%
	Battery Charging	928 hours	(39 days)	18%
	Total Engine Hours (9 years)	5161 hours	(215 days)	100%
Total Engine Hours Per Year 570 hours (24 days)				
2) Diesel Consumption 9300 liter		(1.8 liter per hour)		
The cheapest diesel was in Algeria (US$0.03/liter and Indonesia (US$0.10/liter)				
3) Electricity Consumption:	We had 2x170 amp. deep cycle batteries onboard, one starter battery and one house battery for cabin lights, radar, refrigeration, communications and navigational equipment. Our electricity consumption was approx. 80-90 amp. hours per day. Four solar panels produced approx. 80 amp. hours per day (based on 8-10 hours of sunshine per day). When we were under sail and used both the radar and navigation lights while the fridge was on, the solar panels were not able to produce sufficient electricity. Then we had to run the engine to recharge the house battery.			

75

LAYOVERS - "ON THE HARD"

Nor Siglar was "on the hard" in boat yards six times; four due to winter and/or hurricane/cyclone seasons, maintenance and bottom painting, once to have the bottom painted and once for repairs. The boat yards were in the following countries:

Florida, USA	Fort Lauderdale	Preparations for Atlantic
Norway	Halden *	Bottom painting
Tyrkia	Marmaris *	Winter/ Bottom painting
Trinidad	Chaguramas *	Hurricane season/Bottom painting
Fiji	Vuda Point *	Cyclone season/Bottom painting
Singapore	Raffles Marina	Repairs

* Trip home (by air)

With the exception of Norway, leaving the boat in these places for extended periods was never a problem. The local authorities simply placed the boat "in bond", a formality that just involved signing a few documents at an insignificant sum of money. Upon proof of valid insurance, the marina took over the responsibility of the boat in our absence. In Norway, however, since we wished to leave the boat for more than six months, we were forced to import it and pay Value Added Tax, duty and an engine fee based on HP. Should we decide to leave again in a few years for warmer climes, we will not get a refund.

OTHER LAYOVERS

Guatemala	Rio Dulce *	Hurricane Season
Portugal	Vilamoura *	Trip home
Spain	Sevilla	Winter
Morocco	Mohammedia	Illness

* Trip home (by air)

ANCHORAGES:

Out of a total of 316 anchorages, where we were anchored anywhere from 24 hours to a maximum of two weeks, we only dragged seven times. Only two of these incidents could be considered critical to the safety of the boat.

We carried three anchors onboard: Northill (25 kg), Bruce (15 kg) and Danforth (15 kg). Bruce was our favorite anchor. We carried 50 meters of 5/8" chain and always paid out at least five times the depth. We rarely used more than one anchor at a time. The few times we used two, we got into deep trouble. The reason for this is that during a weather change, the wind has a tendency to shift 180° in no time, while increasing considerably in strength. If it was necessary to weigh anchor in a hurry and move, it was practically impossible to grapple with two anchors simultaneously and quickly without complications. We experienced this a couple of times in the Mediterranean, where anchorages can be quite untenable.

It is a good idea to paint the anchors white. This way, they can easily be seen on the bottom through clear water – in Indonesia on 20 meters depth!

THE SHIP'S LOG

The voyage was duly documented and produced a total of 24 log books of 100 sheets each, i.e. 2400 sheets or 4800 pages! At first we used "Reed's Log Book for Yachts". But this became far too costly. So, after having completed five of those, we created our own. Layout and columns were as follows:

Left-hand page: Date:......... From:............ To:.............

Time | Course | Latitude | Longitude | Log | Wind Speed | Sea Condition | Barometer | Temperature | Distance (log/GPS) | Speed (log/GPS) | GPS "to go" | Engine Hrs.

Right-hand page: Remarks:

On the bottom of each page, we kept a summary of daily and running totals of engine hours, distance and average speed according to both log and GPS. The person coming off watch updated the log, every four hours during the day and every three hours at night, unless conditions demanded it be done more often.

In addition to the "Ship's Log", we kept a "Maintenance Log" in which all equipment was catalogued and the time and type of Maintenance and Repairs noted.

The voyage resulted in over 5000 slides and at least as many regular photos.

WEATHER CONDITIONS

In general, the route was planned and carried out according to information obtained from Jimmy Cornell's "World Cruising Routes", a very useful reference book which contains valuable descriptions regarding ocean routes, distances and the season when the best weather conditions may be expected in the respective areas. This way, we tried to stay within the "safe" latitudes, always striving to be "at the right place at the right time". We were always careful to coordinate our route with optimal weather patterns, i.e. the Pacific (April/May-October) and the Caribbean (November-May). Accordingly, we managed to avoid dramatic weather systems of extreme winds, strong currents and scary wave heights that some circumnavigators' experience.

Apart from some nasty tropical squalls, i.e. brief, torrential rain showers accompanied by winds gusting to storm force strength, we never had winds stronger than 40-45 knots for any length of time. In fact, wind strength of more than 30-35 knots was rare. Consequently, we are unable to brag about having survived numerous storms "with waves as high as buildings"! Gales, yes. Perhaps 4 or 5 of 2-3 days' duration. These were encountered on the West Coast of Nicaragua and Costa Rica, down the coast of Portugal, across the Atlantic a couple of times and up the Red Sea.

Speaking of waves. It is not easy to estimate wave heights. We don't believe we have ever experienced waves higher than 5 meters. They may have seemed higher at times, and other sailors may have thought differently. Have we been lucky? Or could it be that offshore sailors have a tendency to exaggerate?

But at least we can brag about having experienced a hurricane! 70-80 knots, no less! Admittedly, we were safely moored at a dock. However, the fierce winds came up very suddenly and took us completely by surprise. Fortunately, the hurricane only lasted a couple of hours. But this was bad enough, as Martin had just had a back operation. So it was up to me to get the "macho" Muslim men of Morocco, who are not particularly fond of taking orders from "the weaker sex", to assist me with the mooring lines. Fortunately, we escaped with only a scare and a bent stanchion.

Luckily, we did not experience any great disasters on our voyage. We didn't break the mast. We didn't break any rigging. We never capsized. We were, however, always careful to take precautions before the ocean crossings, i.e. secured the stove, lashed down batteries and anchors and put hinges and locks on all hatches and floor boards. Pad eyes were mounted in the cockpit and jack lines stretched along the deck for easy clip-on of safety harnesses. The railing has been under water a few times, but never the boom. The boat has never healed over more than 45°. At times, we took some big seas over the stern and into the cockpit, however never so much that it was ever alarming. We never took on water into the boat through the hull, nor had any serious leakage. We never fell overboard. We never used our life jackets but were always careful to wear our safety harnesses and hooked on during the night and during rough weather.

The best sailing conditions we ever experienced were in the eastern trade winds of the Caribbean, the northwest trade winds along the coast of Portugal, inside the coral reefs of Tonga and in the protected waters of Turkey. The worst and most frustrating sailing conditions we encountered were going north in the Red Sea (northerlies) and in the many notorious wind patterns of the Mediterranean; Levanter and Mistral, Scirocco and Meltemi. The "feast or famine" conditions made sailing there far from ideal. For us, the most stressful leg was the English Channel, with its strong currents and poor visibility, fast crossing ferries and continuous freighter traffic. The longest period of calm was five consecutive days in the South China Sea.

The longest ocean crossings were in the Pacific from Galapagos to Hiva Oa, Marquesas (24 days/2920 nautical miles) and the Atlantic from Gran Canaria to Trinidad (23.5 days and 2982 nautical miles). The fastest passage (6 days/6.3 knot avg.) was from Vancouver to San Francisco (north westerlies) and in the Dutch Antilles (east trade winds), where we actually surfed between the ABC Islands at a speed of 10-12 knots. The 24-hour record was 158 nautical miles – 6.6-knot average. Average speed and distance per 24 hours of the entire circumnavigation: 4.7 knots and 111 nautical miles.

PREPARATIONS

Were we well enough prepared to undertake such a long voyage? Martin, who "was born with salt water in his veins" and grew up sailing on the south coast of Norway, felt quite comfortable with his navigational and sailing skills. What he did lack, however, was experience with diesel engines, modern electronic equipment and everything to do with electricity (AC/DC)! He only took a weekend course in diesel mechanics. Otherwise he learned most of what was needed through technical books and got help from other sailors whenever necessary.

I, on the other hand, had never set foot on a sailboat until I was 38, and knew absolutely nothing about sailing. So I took a bunch of courses - everything from Basic Boating to Seamanship Sail, Advanced Piloting and Ham Radio. Six years before leaving, we moved onboard the boat, first of all to find out if I could become accustomed to life onboard, secondly, to save money and get the boat ready for offshore – and thirdly, most important of all - to find out whether we would be able to live in such close quarters 24 hours a day, 365 days a year.

We both took courses in first aid, radar and celestial navigation. Also, we did a short trial run offshore (VICE 90), to practice reefing and boat handling and to test our "sea legs". Otherwise we read all the literature we could get our hands on with respect to offshore cruising. The most useful articles were written by offshore sailors in the membership publications of various sailing organizations, i.e. Currents and the SSCA Bulletin. When we were underway, we got the information we needed from the "Bibles" of offshore sailors, i.e. cruising guides and hand books for the various cruising destinations, ex. Chris Doyle in the Caribbean, Charlie's Charts in the Pacific, Rod Heikel in the Mediterranean and Imray Lawry just about everywhere else. It was also useful to have tourist guide books onboard, i.e. Lonely Planet, Michelin, Blue Guide, Fodor etc.

In hindsight, we find that most of our mistakes were committed during the first and the last year of our adventure. Obviously, in the beginning, we lacked experience. We also wanted to sail fast and were perhaps somewhat foolhardy, often using too much sail, reefing too late and took off whenever we felt like it, without paying proper attention to the weather forecast. "Surely, it couldn't be that bad?"

After a few mishaps (accidental gybe, injured crew, a near grounding, a nasty fall), we became much more cautious, reefed earlier and waited for favourable weather whenever possible. When friends wanted to visit, they would have to come and join us where we were. After having learned the hard way, battling conditions at sea to meet a deadline, we no longer would risk the safety of the boat, nor ourselves to make a rendezvous in a preplanned place. Normally, it was easier for visitors to reach us by land than it was for us by sea! Schedules and deadlines are the worst enemies of the offshore sailor.

There is no doubt that the hardships endured during the final year of cruising were partially caused by having become somewhat blasé. Running aground in Fiji and Indonesia are classic examples of this phenomenon. Like it or not, after many years out there, one starts to suffer from the "been there, done that, got the T-shirt!"-syndrome.

COMMUNICATION

Loyal supporters ashore looked after our bills, and saw to it that our mail was forwarded at regular intervals, roughly once every 2-3 months. The fact that letters might be several months old by the time we received them was not important. We just loved to receive news from home, even if it was old! At first, we used American Express and various marinas as forwarding address. Otherwise, friends brought the mail when they came to visit. We seldom used Poste Restante, as the post office tends to return mail to sender after only two weeks. That was too risky, since it is very difficult to estimate exact time of arrival way in advance. Plans may change, as can travel routes, depending on weather conditions. During nine years, we only lost one mail parcel. That was in Guatemala.

During the last couple of years, with the on-set of e-mail, the "good old" mail parcels came to an abrupt end. And that was really too bad. The joy one experiences when receiving mail from home at sea, far exceeds the instant excitement one feels when opening the inbox on the screen. Naturally, e-mail is both fast and convenient, so many sailors had it installed on their boats. However, we resisted that temptation, prepared our messages on floppies onboard, and used Internet Cafés ashore instead. We did not want to join the gang of internet cruisers who spend hours on end down below in the lovely hard-to-reach anchorages of paradise…..

We also communicated with family and friends by ham radio and/or telephone ashore. Weather forecasts and invaluable information between offshore sailors was exchanged on the various "cruisers' nets", both on Single Side Band and ham radio. Otherwise, we kept abreast with the world news on CBC, BBC and Voice of America. Cell phones are not useful on the high seas and cannot replace the SSB.

ILLNESS

Most offshore sailors are healthy, and so are we, except for occasional back problems, which have bothered both of us since long before we went offshore. After suffering a slipped disk, Martin had an operation in Morocco. I put my back out five times, making me practically immobile a couple of weeks each time - in Panama, Norway, Greece, Galapagos, and the Maldives. Fortunately, we never became incapacitated by bad backs at the same time!

Other afflictions:

Martin: Tick (Costa Rica), hookworms (Guatemala), urinary infection (Tunisia), infected wart/nail (Galapagos), cuts and scrapes, the biggest one to the head (Indian Ocean).

Anne: Seasickness, eye infections, cuts and scrapes, menopause.

Crew: Deep cut on the leg (Costa Rica – during gale).

We were both bothered by skin infections, a constant problem in the tropics, where seemingly minor cuts and scrapes, contracted while snorkeling on coral reefs, become tender and infected. Thorough disinfecting and a good antibiotic cream would clear it up. To treat severe infections, we kept antibiotics and penicillin onboard. Tylenol 3 and Paralgin Forte were the strongest painkillers we ever needed.

We both suffered food poisoning once; Martin from a piece of veal in a restaurant in Costa Rica, myself, most likely from a bad egg while in the Solomon Islands.

Apart from hookworms, which Martin contracted in the

Guatemalan jungle, allegedly from walking barefoot, our stomachs fared quite well.

Normally, we ate the local food and fresh produce and drank the water unless the locals themselves didn't do it. If we were unsure of the water quality, we added chlorine to it. We never bought bottled water, nor did we boil it, contrary to most offshore cruisers. And actually, it seemed as though our resistance was that much stronger for it. Our feeling and experience is that when traveling so slowly by sailboat, there is plenty of time to get acclimatized. That way one gradually gets used to the local strains of bacteria and has ample opportunity to build up immunity and resistance.

With respect to malaria, we took chloroquin tablets in areas of high occurrence (Solomon Islands and Indonesia). Otherwise, we used mosquito repellant, covered our arms and legs as much as possible, and tried to stay indoors at dusk and dawn, when the malaria mosquito is the most active. We used mosquito netting on all hatch openings and burnt mosquito spirals in the cockpit at night.

The sun is enemy number one of the offshore sailor. We were careful to keep our heads covered, used sunscreen liberally, and stayed in the shade whenever possible. And that was not at all difficult in the heat of the tropics!

We had a well stocked first aid kit onboard, and managed, in general, to cure ourselves. Our first aid equipment was kept in a locker in the bulkhead behind the settee in the main salon. That way, with the patient on the sofa, we had easy access to whatever was needed. When you only have yourself to rely on, you learn to become quite imaginative with experience and as time goes by. When Martin came down with a urinary infection (which we at first thought was a kidney stone attack) underway from Tunisia to Gibraltar, and he couldn't keep the painkillers down, he tried them as suppositories instead. It worked!

Fortunately, we never became seriously ill – no broken bones, no dangerous complications. Naturally, we hurt ourselves from time to time. But the bruises, and scrapes were never so bad that we couldn't take care of them ourselves. At times we did have some dental problems, though. Martin lost half a molar in Mexico, and had a crown put on in Guatemala – a very professional and very cheap job. Myself, I lost an old filling in Egypt and had a temporary crown fitted in Israel – a very professional and very expensive job! We had dental cement onboard for such emergencies. It was a temporary solution and was only meant to last until we reached a dentist. Menopause, believe it or not, had a positive effect on me: I didn't get as seasick as I used to! In fact, it nearly disappeared!

PROBLEMS IN PARADISE

- Weevils and mice, cockroaches and malaria mosquitoes.
- Crocodiles and deadly jellyfish, sharks and sea snakes.
- Thieves and pirates
- Runaways and refugees.

Weevils can be a real problem in the tropics. It is possible to avoid them by storing dry goods (flour, rice, pasta, etc.) in airtight plastic containers with screw-top lids and a couple of bay leaves. The cockroach population was kept to a minimum by using cockroach hotels and bottle caps filled with a mixture of borax, icing sugar and condensed milk. In places known for crocodiles and deadly jellyfish, sharks or sea snakes, we simply did not swim. We managed to escape pirates, mainly by sailing together in flotillas with other boats.

We did not carry any weapons onboard. Instead, we had pepper spray and a strong floodlight by the companionway ready to spray and blind uninvited guests. We also had knives and a couple of baseball bats readily available for self-defense. Fortunately, we never had to use any of this material. To prevent break-ins, we looked after each other's boats and took turns going ashore in places with a bad reputation. We always locked the boat. But this would make no difference to professional thieves. It is not very difficult to break into a boat. Fortunately, we never encountered any refugees or runaways.

WHAT DID IT COST?

We kept detailed records all along and know exactly how much we spent, i.e. US$30,000 per year. There is no doubt that a circumnavigation can be done for less, especially if it is done over a shorter period of time. Also, spending varies from person to person. Our expenditures may be higher than others'. On the other hand, they may also be lower. It all depends on lifestyle, age, habits and personal needs.

Included in our nine-year overall average budget are six trips home by air, a considerable expense that most circumnavigators do not have. Also, we had a lot of visitors - 65 in all. None of them were paying guests. And even though they split the cost of food and treated us from time to time, we still spent more when we had visitors. We had to change our every day lifestyle, which was normally quite frugal. The visitors, on the other hand, were on vacation, and obviously wanted to enjoy themselves, so expenses, especially for beverages, increased. But then we cut corners in other areas. One example was charts. We hardly ever bought new ones, but often exchanged them with other sailors, made photo copies or got them for free. The clothing account was negligible as the wardrobe basically consisted of swimsuits, shorts and t-shirts. Whenever renewals were necessary, they were inexpensive as they were mostly acquired in third world countries. When sightseeing ashore, we rarely rented cars but used the local bus. When staying overnight, we resorted to small, private pensions or one- or two star hotels.

But let's go back to the very beginning: Nor Siglar was delivered new to Vancouver from the Gib'Sea manufacturer in France in 1985, at which time the price tag was US$75,000. Since then, we have spent another US$75,000 to equip her for long-term live-aboard and offshore sailing. Almost half of this was invested in equipment before we left home. (See the Chapter: "Nor Siglar: Pros & Cons of a Circumnavigator".

During the planning stages of our voyage, we estimated an average annual budget of abt. US$18,000, of which boat equipment would be abt. US$3,000 and Maintenance and Repair US$1,500. In actual fact, we ended up using 60% more, i.e. US$30,000 per year, of which equipment was US$6,000 and Maintenance and Repair US$3,000, i.e. twice as much as anticipated. Close to half the budget was spent on:

Boat Equipment (18%), Maintenance and Repair (10%), Boat/Health/Accident Insurance (11%), Harbour Dues (5%), Operating Costs (diesel and propane) (2%) and Cruising fees & Licenses (2%). The remainder consisted of Food, Beverage, and Restaurants (21%), Transportation, Sightseeing and Hotels (11%), Gifts, Souvenirs, and Personal Effects (10%), Charts, Books, Film, Development and Communications Expense (7%), Membership Fees (3%).

Costs could have been significantly lower if we had bought used equipment instead of new, when we needed replacements, and if we had done all maintenance and repair ourselves. But because of our bad backs, we often had to hire help. So although we did all routine maintenance of the boat and engine ourselves, major jobs, i.e. painting of both hull and bottom, was done by locals. We often tried to take advantage of cheap, local labour. However, this did not always pay, as locals often operate according to different principles and a lax schedule, i.e. "island time", something which doesn't always produce a satisfactory result.

Boat insurance is expensive, but we were afraid to be without coverage. Many offshore sailors are on a tight budget and chance to be uninsured. They would rather spend this money on equipment and repair to keep their boat in good condition.

Membership in different sailing associations is, of course, not strictly necessary. However, we feel the benefit of belonging to some of these is well worth the expense. Shops and marinas around the world offer discounts to certain clubs. Besides, excellent membership publications offer useful information to offshore sailors, information that may not be available elsewhere.

The cost of Gifts and Souvenirs, Film and Development, Personal and Clothing can, of course, also be reduced with prudence. Much depends on the type of life style one was used to before leaving home. Frugal people continue to live frugally offshore. Big spenders continue to spend away as well.

Location has a lot to do with the amount of money spent. Europe, including Scandinavia and the Mediterranean, is very expensive, while Central and South America, a number of islands in the South Pacific and most of Asia is very cheap. Australia, New Zealand, French Polynesia, the Caribbean, USA and Canada are moderately expensive. Our budget reflects a whole year in Norway and two in the Mediterranean.

Other reasons why our budget was so underestimated was that the duration of the voyage and distance covered became much longer than planned. Nine years at sea is a long time for a sailboat. The sharp tropical sun, salt water and air and hostile elements at sea take their toll on boat and equipment. After a few years of this, things start to break down. It is expensive to keep an offshore sailboat in good, seaworthy condition, especially over a long period of time.

Our budget is probably not representative of a typical circumnavigation. We were away for a long time, had many visitors, put the boat on the hard and went home by plane six times, and spent considerable time in countries with high living standard (four years out of nine). Other offshore sailors manage on less than us. Then again, there are those that spend much more. But one thing is sure: Gone are the days when you can cruise on US$1,000 per month. We do think, though, that one could carry out a voyage such as ours on around US$22-24,000 per year .

With respect to financing the voyage, we sold our house and a great deal of our belongings and moved onboard Nor Siglar six years prior to take-off. Otherwise, we financed it through income from our wood lot, articles to "Seilas", a Norwegian sailing magazine, private pensions (which we had not planned to touch) and Martin's Government Pension, which he chose to start taking out when he turned 60.

Anne E. Brevig

APPENDIX 3

ABOUT THE AUTHORS

ABOUT THE YACHT NOR SIGLAR

EQUIPMENT

WHAT WORKED / DIDN'T WORK

GLOSSARY TERMS

ABOUT THE AUTHORS
ANNE E. BREVIG AND MARTIN VENNESLAND

Anne grew up in Halden, Norway as a country girl on a farm. She always dreamt of seeing the world and began her adventures with life as an au pair, studying languages in Switzerland, Germany and the USA. In New York, she embarked on a career in international shipping and later became comptroller of a large Norwegian shipping company's Vancouver offices. When Anne met Martin at the age of 38, she was completely new to sailboats.

Having grown up inland, she didn't learn to swim until she was 16, was afraid of the water and became seasick easily. Anne never thought in her wildest imagination that one day she would exchange her comfortable life ashore with the often extreme challenges of life at sea – a decision she has never regretted!

Martin was born with salt water in his blood. He grew up by the tang of the sea in the small village of Sagesund on the south coast of Norway and has sailed all his life. The dream of travelling to exotic and distant shores on his own keel took shape at an early age. As a young man he emigrated to Canada to become a professional forester.

When taking early retirement to venture offshore, Martin was head of one of Canada's largest forestry consultingfirms. An avid outdoors person, he is happiest in the mountains, at his woodlot tending his cedars and Douglas firs or sailing on the high seas.

Nor Siglar in her element

ABOUT THE YACHT NOR SIGLAR

When choosing Nor Siglar, which means Northern Sailor in old Norse, we looked at practical points like size, strength, comfort, standing and running rigging, keel and rudder configuration, sailing ability and, of course, logical safety factors like cockpit draining, size of winches, hatches and windows etc. We did not wish to take a doctor's degree in dynamics or physics to be able to sail a boat around the world, and after having done so, don't think that is necessary either.

After having looked at a variety of sailboats, we finally chose a modern production boat constructed of hand laid fiberglass for the following reasons:

In contrast to the traditional full keeled, heavy displacement designs, we thought a lighter displacement, high performance cruiser-racer would give us superior sailing ability, higher speed and greater comfort. The size would be easy for a middle-aged couple to handle, while providing ample interior space and stowage, and still be large enough for a sea kindly motion.

The low maintenance aspect of a fiberglass boat was a major factor in the decision making process. It is a well-known fact that offshore cruisers spend a lot of time on maintenance and repair to keep their vessels seaworthy. Therefore, keeping these chores to a minimum is very important so that R & R, "Rest & Relaxation", doesn't always turn into a "Repair & Reprovisioning" ordeal instead. Who wants to spend hours on end varnishing wood and fixing hot, leaky teak decks when there are beautiful anchorages and unique cultures to be explored?

With a few exceptions, we have been very satisfied with NOR SIGLAR. Sailing-wise she has performed well in all conditions, which we have encountered. The light displacement, high ratio main and fin keel make her very fast in light winds. She also sails very well high into the wind, which we have found to be extremely important. Contrary to common belief, sailing around the world is not all downwind sailing. This is wishful thinking. Time and again, we have experienced conditions with wind on the nose where it should have been on the stern, even in "so-called" trade wind areas. Gone are the days of predictable weather patterns. Weather systems all over the world are no longer what they used to be.

VESSEL SPECIFICATONS

NOR SIGLAR

Gib'Sea sloop built in 1985
by Gibert Marine, La Rochelle, France

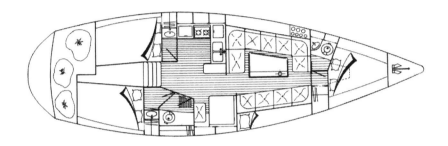

SPECIFICATIONS:

Total length (LOA): 40.4 ft

Hull length (HOA): 38.1 ft

Water line length: 31.8 ft

Beam: 12.5 ft

Draft: 6.5 ft

Mast height: 57.1 ft

Weight (displacement): 17,309 lbs.

Ballast (keel): 7,100 lbs.

SAILS:

Main sail: 355 sq. ft

Cruising spinnaker: 678 sq. ft

No. 1 Genoa (130%): 473 sq. ft

No. 2 Genoa (110%): 398 sq. ft

No. 1 Stay sail: 237 sq. ft

No. 2 Stay sail: 129 sq. ft

Storm jib: 75 sq. ft

Engine: Perkins 4.108 – 50 HP

Fuel tank: 160 litres

Water tanks: 325 litres (1 x 200 l, 1 x 125 l)

EQUIPMENT

STANDARD EQUIPMENT (delivered with the boat):

Fridge, 2-burner propane stove with an oven, pedestal compass, wheel steering, outside bilge pump, 4 electric faucet pumps, 7 Barlow winches (2 self tailing), manual windlass, 1 battery, Perkins 4.108 50 HP engine.

ADDITIONAL EQUIPMENT (acquired later):

110-volt shore-power with charger and 240-volt transformer, house battery, AC/DC inverter, 4 solar panels, wind-generator, wind-vane, electric windlass, digital volt- and ampère meter, battery monitor, water-maker, hot water-heater, diesel-heater, propane system with 2x20-lb. tanks, roller furling on forestay and cutter-stay, collapsible mast steps.

NAVIGATIONAL AIDS:

2 GPS instruments (1 mounted/1 hand-held), 2 sextants with almanac and distance tables, 2 wall-mounted clocks, 1 barometer, 1 radar, 2 binoculars, 2 handheld compasses, foghorn, depth-sounder, wind-speed indicator, knot-metre, charts, reference books and cruising guides world wide.

COMMUNICATIONS EQUIPMENT:

2 VHF radios (1 mounted/1 hand-held), 1 SSB/HAM radio, 1 automatic antenna tuner, 1 AM/FM radio with CD and cassette players, 2 Walkmans.

SAFETY EQUIPMENT:

EPIRB (Emergency Position Indicating Radio Beacon), 6-person life-raft, emergency grab-bag, man overboard pole with light, life ring, life sling harness with line, rescue strobe lights, flares and flare gun, 3 safety harnesses, 6 life-vests, jack lines for safety harnesses mounted on deck, radar reflector, power searchlight, loudhailer, wire-cutter and axe, 3 fire extinguishers, buckets and 3 bilge pumps (1 electric/2 manual), conical plugs adjacent to all sea cocks.

SELF DEFENCE EQUIPMENT:

2 baseball bats, mace, hand-held electric "tazer", companionway alarm. No weapons.

GROUND TACKLE:

1 30 lb. Bruce (80 ft. chain/300 ft. line), 1 50 lb. Northill (205 ft. chain/200 ft. line), 1 30 lb. Danforth (25 ft. chain/200 ft. line) and 1 10 lb. Grapple for the dinghy

DINGHY:

1986-1994: Zodiac 10 ft. rigid bottom rubber dinghy with a 9.9 HP outboard engine

1994- Avon Rollup R 2.85 metre rubber dinghy with a 5 HP outboard engine

SPARES:

Engine parts as recommended in the Perkins Manual, tiller, propeller, whisker-pole, standing rigging, automatic antenna tuner, sheets and halyards, blocks and tackles, nuts, bolts and screws, batteries, light-bulbs, plastic hoses, electrical wiring, spare parts for the heads, sail repair kit with extra canvas.

MISCELLANEOUS:

Tools for electrical and mechanical repairs incl. blocks of wood and plywood sheets for potential damage to hull and hatches, extensive first-aid kit with a multitude of medications; fishing equipment, folding bicycles, scuba-diving equipment, cameras, computer, printer, electric sewing machine, vacuum cleaner, water filter, fuel filter with water separator, multimetre, fans, sun-shower, jerry cans, flashlights, headlamps, signal flags, guest flags, gifts, trading items and the usual personal and household effects.

For more details, see the Seven Seas Adventures website:

www.sevenseasadventure.com

WHAT WORKED / DIDN'T WORK

NOR SIGLAR has now completed her circumnavigation and returned to Norway where she'll serve as our floating summer home and cruiser for several years to come. During her nine years at sea, she logged 56,000 nautical miles (abt. two times around the world), visiting 47 countries and 29 island colonies on the way. In this article, we will tell you a little about NOR SIGLAR, why we chose her as our home for 15 years and our transport around the world for nine. We will illustrate what was done to make her, in our opinion, a suitable and safe offshore cruiser. Also, we will try to explain what we were happy with, what we were not happy with, and what we would do differently if we were to do this voyage again.

When choosing our sailboat, we looked at practical points like size, strength, comfort, standing and running rigging, keel and rudder configuration, sailing ability and, of course, logical safety factors like cockpit draining, size of winches, hatches and windows etc. We did not understand or bother to understand mysteries like STIX (Stability index X) or ISO/DIS 12217-2, AVS (Angle of vanishing stability). We did not wish to take a doctor's degree in dynamics or physics to be able to sail a boat around the world, and after having done so, don't think that is necessary either.

After having looked at a variety of sailboats, we finally chose a modern production boat constructed of hand laid fiberglass for the following reasons:

In contrast to the traditional full keeled, heavy displacement designs, we thought a lighter displacement, high performance cruiser-racer would give us superior sailing ability, higher speed and greater comfort. The size would be easy for a middle-aged couple to handle, while providing ample interior space and stowage, and still be large enough for a sea kindly motion.

We liked the conventional and strong standing rigging of masthead rig with upper and lower shrouds and forward and aft inner shrouds. We did not want the fractional rig with its swept back spreaders because this rig is difficult to tune and far from ideal for main sail trim and chafe during downwind sailing. The fractional rig with its larger main sail is also more difficult to sail off the wind because the big main sail exerts its centre of effort a larger distance away from the yachts centre line. The masthead rig is simple, robust, has lighter loadings and will withstand all manner of abuse. This was later justified while pulling the boat off a reef, partly by heeling her over by the spinnaker halyard.

We also liked the deck-stepped mast since we felt this would be safer if we were to be rolled or dismasted. This type of mast would not break open the cabin top, something which could happen with a keel-stepped mast. Another advantage with a keel-stepped mast is dry bilges, i.e. lots of storage underneath the floorboards.

We liked the rudder configuration protected and strengthened by a skeg. This feature definitely saved us from losing the rudder when we got caught in a huge, commercial fish net in the middle of the Indian Ocean. The boat was virtually hanging by the rudder while we were struggling to cut ourselves loose in an operation that lasted almost 3 hours in 25-knot winds and large seas.

We thought the low, narrow windows would be safer in extreme weather as would the outward hinged hatches, and the fact that there were no engine hatches in the cockpit.

On deck, the cockpit was large and comfortable, while still reasonably safe with a high bridge deck to the companionway and two large, self-draining holes. Below, the forward double V-berth, the large salon and two double cabins aft gave more than enough space for two, and occasionally one or two visitors. We preferred two smaller cabins aft rather than one large Owners' cabin, as one stern cabin could serve as storage space for our full size, folding bikes and other bulky items, while the other would be a comfortable sea berth. While working and living aboard before taking off, one of these cabins was converted into an ideal wardrobe.

The two heads, one on the forward port side and one on the aft starboard side were a great plus. Regardless of tack, one of them was always at a comfortable angle. Besides, in heavy seas, it is good to have a toilet far aft for those who get seasick easily. And if one breaks, there is always a spare. Finally, it is nice to be able to offer guests their own, private toilet.

The low maintenance aspect of a fiberglass boat was a major factor in the decision making process. It is a well-known fact that offshore cruisers spend a lot of time on maintenance and repair to keep their vessels seaworthy. Therefore, keeping these chores to a minimum is very important so that R "&" R, "Rest "&" Relaxation", doesn't always turn into a "Repair "&" Reprovisioning" ordeal instead. Who wants to spend hours on end varnishing wood and fixing hot, leaky teak decks when there are beautiful anchorages and unique cultures to be explored?

IMPROVEMENTS

In order to make NOR SIGLAR better suited and safe for offshore cruising, we made several improvements in the way of additions and modifications. The major ones are as follows:

In the Cockpit:

A permanent aluminum dodger with 3 large safety type glass windows and soft-top sunbrella sunroof with side curtains in clear plastic. This dodger kept us dry in almost any conditions and was strong enough even in heavy weather. In the tropics, we added mesh side curtains all around the cockpit to create shade and shelter from the sun, while still letting the breeze through. While at anchor in hot climates, a long, rectangular, white heavy duty plastic "bimini" sun roof, stored on deck underway, was stretched across the boom from abaft the mast to the aft end of the cockpit. Zippers had to be sprayed and greased regularly.

A stainless steel "roll-bar" across and alongside the dodger to protect it and us from the boom, and also to provide solid support to hang onto when venturing forward in rough conditions.

A stainless steel 1" tubular railing around the cockpit area. A stainless swim ladder astern. Removable canvas lee cloths around the cockpit. Mesh storage bags on cockpit bulkheads for sheets, lines and sundry.

A fair size, folding cockpit table.

3" vinyl-covered foam cockpit cushions (with cotton slip covers for the tropics).

A double arch across the cockpit aft section on which to mount solar panels, GPS antenna, wind generator, fishing rods and brooms, man overboard pole, boat hooks and a lifting mechanism with which to lower the outboard engine onto the dinghy.

A wooden bracket on the stern railing on which to mount the outboard engine.

Three through hull eye bolts to hook on to in the cockpit, one at the top of the companionway, the other two near the steering console. One halogen fire extinguisher in small lazarette.

On deck:

- One additional hand bilge pump at the top of the companionway steps.
- Two granny bars, one on each side of the mast, to protect us during reefing and other chores on deck. These also provided an excellent platform for the look-out in reef-strewn waters, and a great storage spot for the fenders.
- Two sets of jack lines running from the cockpit to the forestay made of strong, flat, mountain climber's webbing.
- Lazyjacks and radar reflector Two running back stays to stabilise and strengthen the mast.
- Roller furling on both forestay and intermediate forestay.
- Collapsible mast steps to make it easier and safer to be hoisted/go aloft.

Below deck:

- Two fire extinguishers
- A watertight compartment under the forward V-berth as protection against possible collision with whales, containers or any other potential objects floating in the sea.
- A pilot berth in the salon was converted to make room for more locker space and shelving.
- Latches with lock mechanism on all floorboards and salon settees in case of rollover/capsize.
- Lee clothes on both port and starboard salon settees.
- Two wide, padded straps for support; one across the galley, one by the chart table.
- Canvas snap covers on all hatches behind the salon settee cushions to prevent items from falling out when healing over in rough seas.
- Softwood conical plugs secured with string near all through-hull fittings.
- Two halogen fire extinguishers, one at the top of companion/one near the galley

ADDITIONAL EQUIPMENT

Most of this equipment was acquired and/or installed before we left Vancouver (1), although some was added on the way (2):

(1) Installed before we left Vancouver:

- Echo sounder
- wind and boat speed indicators
- wind vane
- wind generator
- electric windlass
- water maker
- hot water heater
- diesel heater
- propane system
- radar
- 2 sextants
- GPS (fixed)
- VHF (fixed)
- AM/FM radio/cassette player
- SSB/Ham radio
- 2 clocks
- 1 barometer
- epirb
- 6 person life raft
- 10 foot rigid bottom rubber dinghy with a 9.9 HP outboard engine

(2) Added on the way:

- 4 solar panels
- inverter (AC/DC)
- amp-monitor
- GPS (handheld)
- VHF (handheld)
- CD player

In order to be as self contained as possible and to make life at sea as safe and comfortable as we could, we also carried a variety of other items:

MISCELLANEOUS EQUIPMENT:

First Aid Kit
(including a wide variety of pharmaceutical supplies and medications)

Safety Equipment:

- life ring/sling/vests
- rescue strobe lights
- flares
- flare gun
- safety harnesses
- "grab bag"
- halogen fire extinguishers
- axe
- wire cutters
- buckets
- loudhailer
- a 400,000 capacity power search light
- man overboard pole
- man overboard strobe light

Self-defense Equipment:

- baseball bats
- maze
- portable alarm system
- We did not carry weapons

Ground Tackle:

We carried four anchors with chain and lines:

- A 25 kg Northill (Fisherman) with 55 m chain/100 m line,
- a 15 kg Bruce with 20 m chain/100 m line,
- a 15 kg Danforth with 20 m chain/75 m line and
- a small 2 kg Grapnel for the dinghy.

In the beginning, we used the Northill as our main anchor and the Bruce as our stern anchor. Later, after having dragged several times, we changed to the Bruce with 55 meters of chain as our main and the Danforth as our stern anchor. We found the Bruce to be an excellent anchor, although we would have preferred it a little heavier. 20 kg would have been ideal. The Northill also provided good holding, however, the chain had a tendency to get caught up in its long pin if/when the boat turned around 360 degrees. It is interesting to note that out of a total of 300 anchorages, we dragged only 7 times. And only two of these incidents could be considered dangerous for the safety of the boat. Apart from the crowded harbours of the Mediterranean, the stern anchor was seldom used, unless we needed to keep the boat into the wind and ocean swell.

Navigational Equipment:

- hand held compasses
- binoculars
- sextants
- charts
- reference books and guides world-wide
- signal flags
- national flags
- signal horns

Spare Parts:

These included tools for all types of electrical and mechanical ship's and rig repair, bits of wood and sheets of plywood for carpentry and hull repair and kits for sail and toilet repair including material and hoses.

- engine spares according to Perkins manual
- emergency tiller for manual steering
- a custom made spare propeller
- extra sheets and halyards
- ropes and lines

- manual and electric water bilge pumps
- whisker poles
- the old standing rig
- fishing gear
- fuel separator,
- 6 fuel and 2 water jerry cans,
- miners lamps and flashlights,
- batteries and bulbs,
- fans and solar shower,
- multimeter and battery tester,
- wind scoop
- odds and ends

Personal Gear:

- cameras
- walkmans
- CDs and cassette tapes
- laptop computer and printer
- electric sewing machine
- 12 Volt vacuum cleaner
- folding bikes
- scuba diving and snorkelling equipment
- bedding and clothing
- back packs and sleeping bags
- kitchen utensils
- books
- pictures
- gifts
- trading items
- "stuff" for personal use

By the time all of this was stowed, including staple provisions for several months at sea, the waterline had to be raised several inches!

POSITIVE ASPECTS

With a few exceptions, we have been very satisfied with NOR SIGLAR. Sailing-wise she has performed well in all conditions, which we have encountered. The light displacement, high ratio main and fin keel make her very fast in light winds. She also sails very well high into the wind, which we have found to be extremely important. Contrary to common belief, sailing around the world is not all downwind sailing. This is wishful thinking. Time and again, we have experienced conditions with wind on the nose where it should have been on the stern, even in "so-called" trade wind areas. Gone are the days of predictable weather patterns. Weather systems all over the world are no longer what they used to be.

Another positive feature with the Gib'Sea is that when the sails are properly set, the boat is well balanced with no weather helm. This is evident from the fact that rudder, shaft and steering mechanisms are still the originals after 56,000 nautical miles. Further, the boat must be well built since there is no sign of any hull or interior bulkhead movements or leaks anywhere. All doors and cupboards are still totally in place, no signs of movements or warping. After hitting a reef in Indonesia at 4 knots and having survived considerable abuse from the towing off and rescuing operation, there are no signs of the keel separating from the hull, nor damage to rig, mast or rudder.

After 15 years, mostly on the water, there are no signs of blisters anywhere on the hull. We did think we had blisters at one time, however, it only turned out to be bubbles between gel coat and antifouling. This was probably due to the fact that the bottom was never sealed properly to begin with, i.e. at the time it was commissioned from factory.

When the boat was 10 years old, all standing rigging was replaced, but only because our insurance company required it. The old rig showed no signs of wear and tear anywhere. As a matter of fact, the bulk of our running rigging, incl. halyards and most mooring lines, sheets and shackles are still the originals and show little sign of chafing. Only the main sheet has been replaced. This is obviously a result of having been conscientious with sheet adjustments and protection on the mooring lines.

Of all the original sails, we have only had to replace the main. After 9 years of constant use and having torn it three times, we exchanged it with a Bainbridge Dacron sail with RT-design and radial cut. This has been an excellent sail. It has kept its shape very well, which is quite amazing after 38,000 nm, mostly in the tropics. This sail with its full battens gave us considerably better speed and pointing capability than our original short batten sail. With its three deep reefs, the third one only used a couple of times, we have never felt the need for a try sail.

Before we left home, we had all foresails re-cut on the high side to make them suitable for ocean sailing. Safety was considered more important than speed. Therefore, we did not invest in a spinnaker either, but brought an easy-to-handle asymmetric gennaker with sock instead. Surprisingly, we only used this sail a few times, as even relatively small ocean waves would create havoc with it, rendering it ineffective and frustrating to use. We have been happy with the furling forestays and would not go offshore with hanked-on sails. Going forward to reduce sails during adverse conditions is probably the most dangerous task on a small boat at sea. The life of our sails was extended by strengthening them with tape in exposed areas and by putting Styrofoam protection on shrouds and spreaders, an effective measure in preventing chafe.

NEGATIVE ASPECTS

The very worst drawback with NOR SIGLAR is the poor access to her engine. It is very difficult to get to the sides and back of it and the propeller shaft stuffing box. In an emergency situation, this could be a dangerous fault. Also, it is impossible to reach the fuel tank to drain and/or clean it.

Further, we discovered two construction weaknesses. The beam across the cabin top that supports the mast on top of the compression post is not one solid piece or section. At one point, it started to move sideways and had to be bolted to the deck to prevent it from "slipping" further. Also, we had to strengthen the deck connection to the bulkhead under the genoa fair lead track since the deck here was "lifting" in very strong winds.

Another very awkward feature is that it is almost impossible to lead wires from the batteries in the cockpit lazarette to the electric board in the main cabin and forward to the bow. There should be conducts for electric wires built into the bulkheads at the time of construction.

In the galley, the counters are too low and the sinks too shallow. Not only does this design reduce storage space below, but is hard on the back. In the cockpit, one of the two lazarette hatches is too large and could be torn off in a roll-over situation. It should be strengthened with larger hinges. We added extra hinges and kept both hatches locked at sea to prevent them from flying open in rough seas.

Also, the two water tanks are too large. They should be divided into several smaller compartments to lessen the noise from sloshing water and safeguard the water supply in case of leakage.

The boat was delivered with electric water pumps in all cabins, heads and galley. We soon realised that this system would use far too much electricity and water and shifted to a manual foot pump in the galley and disconnected all the others.

The double bunk in the aft cabin was too wide as a sea berth. In heavy weather, we had to wedge ourselves in with cushions to keep from rolling sideways. Also, it was poorly ventilated and too hot. The best place to sleep for maximum air and minimum motion was either on the salon floor or settees.

EQUIPMENT WE HAVE BEEN SATISFIED WITH

The Scanmar Monitor windvane has steered the boat practically all the time except when motoring in no wind. Even when motor-sailing in light winds, did we use our faithful "Styrmann". We did not feel that we needed an autopilot until towards the end, when we encountered long periods of calm in the South China Sea. However, today we would recommend a small tiller steering Autohelm 800 (or similar) attached to the wind steering mechanism

The Power Survivor water maker has worked without any problems on and off over the 9 years despite having been "put to bed" for long periods at a time. Even though it only produces 4 litres per hour, it is a nice piece of equipment to have in reserve.

The Icom 735 SSB/ham radio, Furuno 1830 Radar, Magellan Nav 1000 plus GPS (1991), Silva wind, log and depth instruments, BP and Siemens solar panels were all dependable and easy to use, requiring little or no maintenance.

The propane gas system was safe and reliable. Balmar 120 diesel heater. After having been out of service for 6 years, it started up easily Epirb Category 2 ACR, annual battery checks only.

Surrett deep cycle 170-amp hrs. batteries – excellent – lasted 7 years.

Last, but not least, we must not forget our trustworthy diesel engine, Mr. Perkins. We chose Perkins 4.108 because of its size (50 HP) and its excellent reputation of reliability, ruggedness and the good chance of obtaining spare parts for it all over the world. It is very important to have the extra horsepower that can drive an oversized, fixed propeller in heavy wind, current and seas, and to be able to stop the boat fast, if so required. The engine now has 6000 hours on it and still runs like a dream. It has never given us any significant problems. No major repairs have been necessary, only regular service and steady, good maintenance, like changing oil and filters, as per the manual. Being poor mechanics, we were extremely meticulous. Always concerned about dirty diesel, we never filled the tank directly from the pump, but always from jerry cans, using a 3-part filter and adding an anti-contaminant/condensation solution to the fuel. We were also careful to run the engine at its most comfortable revolutions.

EQUIPMENT WE HAVE REPLACED OR BEEN DISSATISFIED WITH

Our major equipment has lasted much better than expected. But although we have been very conscientious and consistent with good maintenance, there are a few exceptions:

The wind generator. We could never get the Four Winds, our "Vivaldi", properly balanced. Further, after only 4 years of use, it corroded so badly that we had to throw it away.

The electric windlass. The Simpson Lawrence Seawolf also corroded very quickly. Besides, it was highly over-rated with respect to its load capacity. We would highly recommend getting one much stronger than suggested by the supplier.

The original 12-volt refrigerator endured 10 years of steady use. It was only after it could not keep up with the heat in the tropics that we had to replace it. On the advice from a fellow sailor, we chose a 12 volt "Super Cool" from Sweden. We were disappointed to find this unit highly over-rated. In the tropics, it could never keep the temperature below 20C(. It served us very poorly for only 3 years when we had to discard it and install yet another one, the third in 14 years.

So far, after 1-O years, the Nova Cool, made in Vancouver, has worked very well. The original stove, a two-burner Eno, was replaced after 12 years of constant use. We chose a Force Ten made in Vancouver, which we have been pleased with so far.

Our first tender, a 10-foot Zodiac rigid bottom dinghy, gave us an awful lot of grief. Firstly, the rubber was of a very poor quality and came apart at the seams even though we used a canvas cover on it in the tropics. So after hours and hours of fixing and innumerable times of gluing, we just gave it away. It was then only 8 years old. Another drawback with the Zodiac was that with its rigid bottom, it was far too heavy for us to manhandle, especially with its large 9.9 HP outboard engine. Therefore, we replaced the engine with a 5HP Mariner and the dinghy with a smaller and lighter Avon 2.85 rollup. We have been very pleased with this combination. We seldom roll up the dinghy for ocean crossings but leave it inflated on the foredeck where it is safely squeezed and secured under the jacklines, which, at the same time, makes these nice and tight to hook on to. We have never had any incidents with the dinghy being in the way, nor of it being in danger of getting washed overboard. To ensure that it stayed securely in its place while underway, it was regularly checked and inflated.

The toilets. We had more trouble with the heads than any other equipment on the whole boat, maybe since we had so many visitors. So we would recommend spending the extra dollar and install top quality heads from the start. Both toilets have been repaired over and over again and were eventually replaced completely.

We have often been asked which equipment we could have done without, and which we would not have left home without.

We could have done without the watermaker as we didn't use it very much (although it gave us peace of mind).

The wind generator was never missed after we discarded it, as the solar panels generated enough electricity for our needs.

We could also have done without the scuba gear, hot water heater and built-in shower. On the other hand, we feel we could not have done without the GPS, windvane, SSB/ham radio, radar, electric windlass, fridge, liferaft and epirb.

Many cruisers had a freezer, TV/VCR, weather fax, inmarsat, autopilot, generator, huge fuel tank(s), and lately, e-mail – all gear we did not miss. As a matter of fact, the items which seemed to give people the most grief, were freezers and autopilots which caused endless frustration and delays waiting for mechanics or parts.

As far as we were concerned, we enjoyed sampling the local foods, got more than enough entertainment from the adventure itself and, in general, waited for the wind, rather than firing up the engine every time the speed dropped below 5 knots.

We received all the weather forecasts and cruising information we needed via our SSB/ham radio, with which we also kept in touch with other boats through various nets and, thanks to landbased amateurs, family and friends at home.

Ashore, e-mail was accessible from Internet cafes or phone booths via laptop and acoustic coupler.

WHAT WOULD WE HAVE DONE DIFFERENTLY?

Not much, really. We probably should have had a tricolour mast headlight. The radar could have had a shorter range. At times we wished we had known more about diesel mechanics and the mystery of electricity. However, having said that, in hindsight we probably escaped major trouble partly due to our lack of expertise. It was absolutely imperative for us to be extremely meticulous at all times, especially with lay-up of boat and engine, precisely because we had such poor knowledge of diesel mechanics! Anyway, when necessary, we were always able to get help from fellow cruisers. There are so many capable people out there who are more than willing and able to help. Some even make a living from fixing other cruisers' boats. So dreamers should be pleased to know that it is not necessary to be a world champion in everything to manage offshore. As a matter of fact, in our view, plain, ordinary horse sense will get you a long way!

Looking at NOR SIGLAR today, it is hard to believe that she has covered so much ground and gone through so much. Despite having received her fair share of gales and calms, abuse and hardship from the elements offshore, she looks just as good today as when we cut the lines nine years back. So what is the secret? It can be said with one word: Maintenance! And there is no doubt: We have escaped potential trouble because the boat has been in tiptop shape all the time. The stainless steel has not been allowed to rust, the standing rig has been tuned and checked regularly, the running rig kept tight and trimmed, no banging halyards or sheets, new ideas and improvements have been implemented on the way. And we definitely credit our lack of "disasters" to the liberal use of metal polish, WD40, CRC, lube oil and duct tape! In short, NOR SIGLAR is in shape to start another tour around the world any time.

There has always been a lot of writing about what makes a perfect offshore cruiser. In conclusion, we can only confirm that there is no such thing. No boat is perfect. There always seems to be a balancing act, a compromise situation involved and, of course, for most of us, a budget to consider. Therefore, one sees all kinds of boats out there. And when it comes right down to it, all kinds of crafts do manage on the high seas, something, which cannot be said for their crew. Apart from the obvious, i.e. a solid knowledge of sailing, it is the relationship between skipper and crew, which makes or breaks the dream. And the best ingredients for its success, in our opinion, is mutual respect, a healthy portion of self reliance and mental stability, lots and lots of patience and last but not least, just plain, old-fashioned kindness towards one another.

Do we have any advice for the dreamers at home? Just read and learn as much as possible before taking off and equip your vessel with as much as you can afford. While there is a lot to be said for the KISS principle ("keep it simple, stupid"), the more conveniences and comfort you surround yourself with, the more you will enjoy your cruise. But don't try to get it all done before leaving home, cause then you'll never get away! A lot can be done underway. Finally, be careful, reef early and keep your harness on. Guts and a big portion of good luck would also help. And don't forget:

Never leave port on a Friday!

GLOSSARY TERMS

Abeam: At right angles to the keel of a ship

Bilge: The lowest inner part of a ship's hull

Bulkhead: A structural wall which divides the vessel into compartments

Celestial Navigation; Taking positions by measuring the angle of celestial bodies above the horizon using a sextant and then calculating the vessel's location with distance tables and a nautical almanac

Channel 16: Emergency channel on VHF radio

Cockpit: A recessed part of the deck in which to sit and steer

Cutter Stay: An inner forestay for a smaller sail

Dragging: When an anchor slides along the bottom

EPIRB: Emergency Position Indicating Radio Beacon

Forepeak: A space (normally a cabin) in the bow of the vessel

Furling Gear: Equipment used to enable sails to be rolled on a stay or boom for storage

GPS: Global Positioning System uses satellite signals to pinpoint locations

Gybe: To change course in a following wind. Sails are moved from one side of the boat to the other. An accidental gybe is when this is not accomplished in a controlled manner. It can be a dangerous manoeuvre.

Halyard: A rope or wire for hoisting sails

Head: Ship's toilet

Lazy-jacks: Lines to contain the mainsail while it is being lowered

Lee Cloth A canvas secured at the side of a berth to keep the occupant from falling out when the boat is healing over or rolling from side to side

Leech: The trailing edge of a sail

Lee Shore: Windward side of a coast or shore

Lee Side: Side of the boat away from the direction of the wind

Lie a Hull A technique used in heavy weather with all the sails down and the tiller lashed to leeward

Life Line: Lines secured along the decks of the boat to prevent people from falling overboard

Mayday: International distress call

Port Side: The left hand side of a boat when looking forward

Preventer: Line leading forward to hold the boom at right angles to the boat when going downwind to prevent a gybe

Pulpit: Railing around the bow of the boat

Quarter: Area between the beam (midship) and the stern of a vessel

Reach: Sailing with the wind on the beam with the sail approximately halfway out. Can be a close reach, beam reach or broad reach

Reefing: To reduce the size of a sail

Running: To sail with the wind behind the boat

Sheet: A line used to adjust the sails

Shrouds: Wire supports on either side of the mast

Spreaders: Short struts between mast and shrouds to add support to the rig

SSB: Single Side Band – short-wave radio

Starboard: The right-hand side of a vessel when looking forward

Stay: A wire, supporting the mast fore and aft

Stern: The rear part of a boat

Tacking: To change course when sailing against the wind

Traveller: A sliding fitting which travels on a track, used to alter the sheeting angles of a sail

Turnbuckle: A mechanism to tighten shrouds and stays

VHF: Very High Frequency radiotelephone used over shorter distances to other vessels or land based stations

Waypoint: A planned crossing point between a certain degree of latitude and longitude

Wind Vane: A device that automatically steers a boat at a preset angle to the wind

Whisker Pole: A pole used to hold out foresails when sailing downwind Windward Direction from which the wind is blowing.

1 nautical mile (nm): 1,852 metres (6,076 feet)

1 knot: 1 nautical mile per hour

1 degree of latitude (°): 60 nautical miles

1 degree of longitude (at equator): 60 nautical miles

1 minute (') of latitude: 1 nautical mile (60' in 1° latitude)

Circumference of the earth at equator: 21,638 nautical miles / 40,075 km

BEAUFORT WIND SCALE

Beaufort Windspeed Description: - Force - Knots

0: - *0* - **Calm**

1: - *1 - 3* - **Light air**

2: - *4 - 6* - **Light breeze**

3: - *7-10* - **Gentle breeze**

4: - *11-16* - **Moderate breeze**

5: - *17-21* - **Fresh breeze**

6: - *22-27* - **Strong breeze**

7: - *28-33* - **Near gale**

8: - *34-40* - **Gale**

9: - *41-47* - **Strong gale**

10: - *48-55* - **Storm**

11: - *56-63* - **Violent storm**

12: - *63+* - **Hurricane**

We met people from all corners of the world, experienced the delight of bonding with fellow cruisers, brushed up on history and language skills and learned about other cultures. We can to know and understand lifestyles completely different from our own and learned that it is possible to live quite happily in a variety of ways in this complex and fascinating world

Anne

Manufactured by Amazon.ca
Bolton, ON